Battled & Bruised

STILL STRONG, STILL STANDING

Clarence Crayton III

TRILOGY CHRISTIAN PUBLISHERS
Tustin, CA

Trilogy Christian Publishers
A Wholly Owned Subsidiary of Trinity Broadcasting Network
2442 Michelle Drive
Tustin, CA 92780

Battled & Bruised

Copyright © 2024 by Clarence Crayton III

Scripture quotations marked ESV are taken from the ESV® Bible (The Holy Bible, English Standard Version®), copyright © 2001 by Crossway Bibles, a publishing ministry of Good News Publishers. Used by permission. All rights reserved. Scripture quotations marked NKJV are taken from the New King James Version®. Copyright © 1982 by Thomas Nelson. Used by permission. All rights reserved. Scripture quotations marked KJV are taken from the King James Version of the Bible. Public domain.

All rights reserved, including the right to reproduce this book or portions thereof in any form whatsoever.

For information, address Trilogy Christian Publishing

Rights Department, 2442 Michelle Drive, Tustin, Ca 92780.

Trilogy Christian Publishing/TBN and colophon are trademarks of Trinity Broadcasting Network.

For information about special discounts for bulk purchases, please contact Trilogy Christian Publishing.

Trilogy Disclaimer: The views and content expressed in this book are those of the author and may not necessarily reflect the views and doctrine of Trilogy Christian Publishing or the Trinity Broadcasting Network.

10 9 8 7 6 5 4 3 2 1

Library of Congress Cataloging-in-Publication Data is available.

ISBN 979-8-89333-149-3

ISBN 979-8-89333-150-9 (ebook)

Dedication

To my brother Garrett "G'Money,"
I miss you every day.
To my children, Tyler and Kellen, you are my inspiration, and you have been since the day you were born.

Acknowledgments

I am forever grateful for all these individuals who took hours to pour into me the many encouragements over many days, many weekends, many months, and the many years that helped make this memoir come to life. The constant love and support you special individuals provided, through the tears of therapy, the laughter around the table, and the long talks, were the motivation to my spirit to get back up from the dust and reach for the destiny that God has placed in me. You allowed me to be comfortable, to be vulnerable, and to share the insights of my growth, from my failures to my strengths in life! So, I would like to send a special thank you and an H2P (Hail to Pitt)!

Dr. Clarence & Josephine Crayton
(Dad/Mom)
Terron & Letrice Sumpter
(The Sumpter Crew)

Chris Crayton
Terry & Sui Murphy Family
Tony & Kelly Grano
Rob & Peggy Blanc
The University of Pittsburgh
The R.I.S.E. Church of Oceanside
The Los Angeles Chargers Organization

Contents

Introduction. Battled & Bruised to Be a Blessing!
Turn Stones into Steps ix

Prologue xv

Section 1. In the Beginning

Chapter 1. Gifted to Be Gifted 3
Chapter 2. PK: The Other Side of the Calling 12
Chapter 3. The Crayton Brothers Uniqueness
to the Game 25

Section 2. Getting Prepared for the Show

Chapter 4. Make Your Own Stardom 45
Chapter 5. The Freshman Phenom a Heart
Conditioned 54
Chapter 6. The Cracking Walls of the World 90

Section 3. The Trials and the Evil of Days

Chapter 7. When Tragedy Strikes 147
Chapter 8. Anointed in the Middle 156
Chapter 9. Silence in the Face of Injustice 171
Chapter 10. Place of Conflict to the Place of
Calling 198

About the Author 201

Introduction

BATTLED & BRUISED TO BE A BLESSING! TURN STONES INTO STEPS

There is hope and a future.

Some may find it difficult to believe because from the moment we draw our first breath, life comes assembled with disappointment, with challenging experiences, and with painful events.

I have learned that life creates opportunities for us to trust the Lord our God, not only with our lives but also to trust Him to be with us while we face all that this life brings.

God, the Father, does not take the time to form and cover us while in our mothers' wombs, only to desert us when we are born. I believe He works at making us exactly how He needs us to be in preparation for all that we will encounter in each of our generational lifetimes.

In all of my personal battles and in all the bruises from those battles, my soul prospered because God has always had me in His hands. Through my trust in Him, my faith grew in Him, and my intimate walk deepened with Him. My hope is that as you turn these pages, you take a soulful stroll from a glimpse of my life's accomplishments, lessons, trials, and sufferings that leads you to an intersection where you meet up with the Lover of your soul and that you allow Him to reveal the purpose behind your battles and why He allowed your bruises. Consider this well-known song, Psalm 139:13–14 (KJV), "For thou hast possessed my reins: Thou hast covered me in my mother's womb. I will praise thee; for I am fearfully and wonderfully made: Marvelous are thy works; And that my soul knoweth right well."

The word "reins" in the Hebrew language is referred to as "kidneys." According to Hebrew psychology, the reins are the seat of the deepest emotion and affection of human beings, which God alone can fully know. The two primary functions of the kidneys are to remove waste products from the blood and to help control your blood pressure. And the seat of our emotions and affections is our heart. When the kidneys don't work well, it puts undue pressure on the heart, which most often leads to heart disease.

This psalm tells us that God possessed and purchased our inner parts, our lives, with the blood of Jesus Christ when He gave His life for ours. When we accept Jesus as our Lord and Savior, we receive a spiritual blood transfusion, and all the waste of the sin we have done and will do is removed. Trusting God's promise through Jesus eases and replaces the pressure of life's battles and bruises.

Our journeys in life will include a pinch of obstacles, a cupful of goodness with a dash of difficult experiences that, when heated up in the oven of circumstance, will all add up to a divine recipe.

A recipe that prepares us under the proper conditions sets us up to come face to face with our respective destinies that God planned before the foundation of the world, before all of us were a blip on a sonogram in our mothers' wombs.

No one will escape experiencing tragedies in life, whether they come from the expectations from within or from others or unforeseen events... Evil days will come to us all. The question then becomes, "Will you be ready when that day arrives for you?"

I will be very open and foretelling in the chapters about this story of my life and overcoming my personal battles. I will not be ashamed of the bruises acquired, whether from my obedience or as a result of my disobedience. God used both for His glory!

The challenge comes when people see the glory but never read the pages of the story that produced it. Many see all the things that I may have accomplished in my life, past or present, and may have assessed and evaluated me, my life, and my worth on the basis of the outward glow.

But little did they know that I wasn't "living the glamorous life..." I was going through many, many internal trials.

The truth is, while I looked like I had no cares in the world and portrayed so many of my successes, I was facing battles in my mind in the areas of self-worth, depression, criticism, lack, love, acceptance, pride, and lust. These were no small skirmishes.

Many of these internal conflicts had me on the verge of losing my mind and my peace, but God's voice was always on the other side of the fight, calling me out and drawing me near.

I was physically bruised with injuries and drained from emotional stress. My body went through many different types of physical pain, including the process of being diagnosed with a disease that gives you an average of only fifteen days to remain on this earth to live. I was diagnosed with diabetes at the prime of my athletic career. I experienced mental and emotional stress... from missing out on my dream of the NFL, the mental torture from losing loved ones, bad relationships, and some devastating racial and racist acts that occur against my culture took a toll on me. It is only God with His healing power to whom I give the glory through my near-death experience and another dealing with racism to the degree that it almost cost me my life.

By the time you finish reading this book, I desire for you to have the end game I was blessed to experience, and that is in spite of the very difficult struggles and attacks that brought with them physical and mental torture, but I am still strong, and I am still standing!

James 1:12 (KJV) says, "Blessed is the man that endureth temptation: for when he is tried, he shall receive the crown of life, which the Lord hath promised to them that love him."

I outlasted the trials, and I passed a faith test!

I let Jesus Christ fully take over my life and then engaged my faith to get up when the challenges and fights knocked me down.

I am still strong. God never left my side. As a PK (pastor's kid), I had always been in touch with God. I had this firm foundation in me to fight through tough times with the hope of Him inside of me that allowed me to continue on no matter what.

As with the three Hebrew boys, Shadrach, Meshach and Abednego, in Daniel 3:19–30, God showed up in the conflict they had with King Nebuchadnezzar's decree. God was with them in their fiery trial. So had I called on the same God, in the name of Jesus, as I was going through my battles, getting beat up and bruised. And like these three witnesses, I don't look like what I have been through, and I thank God for the privilege to be

His witness to you of His power over everything meant to destroy you.

I am still standing.

Consider Joseph, who was betrayed by his brothers and ultimately sold off and ended up in prison, being left for dead like the man who was cared for by the good Samaritan or chased into a cave like King David.

Similarly, we can find confidence in the knowledge of the prize they received at the end of their battles and bruises.

Through my story, I want to paint a picture of the human emotional struggle and the victory that awaits the one who does not faint or get weary but endures the battles and bruises and allows them to be the catalyst to help others.

I pray my journey inspires you to never quit and never lose hope. We all have stories of the hardships we go through. Just know you are never alone.

Revelation 12:11 (KJV): "And they overcame him by the Blood of the Lamb, and by word of their testimony; and they loved not their lives unto the death."

Prologue

On a Sunday afternoon during my junior year of high school, I heard my mom scream out from the kitchen, "Tray, come down here!" We had just gotten home from church, as we did every Sunday, and I had gone upstairs to change from my church attire into athletic sweats.

I ran downstairs to see what was going on. My siblings came into the kitchen, too, where we saw my mom standing in front of the phone and the answering machine that hung on the wall. The answering machine blinked. Forty-two messages.

She looked at me and said, "Listen to this." She pressed the button and all forty-two messages were from recruiting coordinators for all the top coaches and schools around the country, and we listened to each one, back-to-back-to-back. We all just looked at each other and knew that this was it. My dream of playing Division 1 football was real. My high school recruitment was unprecedented in our family, even though my brothers and many cousins were talented athletes, too. I was a preseason five-star high school All-American—every player's dream.

Section 1:
In the Beginning

"Who you are inside is what helps you make and do everything in life."

—Mister Fred Rogers

CHAPTER 1

Gifted to Be Gifted

My mother often told me a story of the time when I was two years old and when my parents realized there was something distinct and peculiar about the talent that was within me. My dad, who was an athlete at his own core, played football and basketball, but his true love was track and field. He was a track star in high school. He starred in the 100 meters, 100-meter hurdles, 200 meters, 400 meters, and the relays. He coached my siblings and me in all the sports that we played growing up until junior high and high school, but being a track coach was his favorite. My dad was very gifted in scouting talent because he was also a scout for the Oceanside, CA, sports athletic community.

On the weekends, both my parents would take all of my four siblings and me to the local high school to play and run around the facility. By way of a small crack in the fence, we would squeeze our way in to play on the handball courts and run around the complex to blow off energy as a way of giving our family of seven a chance to get out of the small apartment we were all living in at the time.

While the family was playing on the handball and tennis courts, I slipped away from the group and made my way to the track. Being like most moms, when she noticed I was off on my own away from the pack, my mom wanted my dad to go retrieve me from running around the track, but my dad convinced her it would be a good thing to leave me to it, as it was a surefire way to get me exhausted before we headed home.

There I was, a tiny two-year-old making strides around an official high school track and field. They watched me turn the first corner of the track, my legs striding and pushing like I had done this before in a prior life or something. Then, I was halfway around the track when my parents started to switch their demeanors and look at each other and declare, "Is he going to make it around the entire track?!" Yes, I strode my two-year-old legs around and did a 400-meter run from start to finish.

Not only did I make it once, but I was also going to attempt to go for 800 meters or more. Was I already trying to obliterate going after a personal best and do it again? Could I do it again? We will never know because my mom had my dad run over to get me before I could get lap number two under my belt. I can't recall, but I know my siblings and I left the school grounds right after that because my parents knew it was just a matter of time before I would conk out.

When my parents got home, they talked about how astonished they were at seeing the heart and stamina I demonstrated while running around the track, how I had pushed myself beyond my limit, and as a baby, displayed a special desire for pushing myself beyond the mental limits that would be my calling when it came to sports and life. They already saw a desired heart that circulated through my blood at such a young age. This is a memory my mom would remind me of constantly throughout my athletic career. She would remind me that I was destined by God to do great things, that I was gifted with heart and my desire to push myself through any and all limits life might try to bring. My parents were so encouraging, and that was because they had great examples from their upbringing.

My father came from a big family. Not big, huge. He was the second eldest of eleven brothers and sisters, most all living in Oceanside or a surrounding city. So, as you might imagine, we had gigantic family gatherings at my papa's house. It was his dream to keep his family close together.

My grandparents taught all their children to look out for each other at all costs, from the oldest to the youngest. The motto of "family comes first," although not originating from us, felt so. The number one rule of the Crayton household, which was passed down to the children, was "family over everything."

Seeing all my cousins was an amazing highlight of my youth. We had upwards of one hundred people or more at almost every holiday gathering. It was like having constant family reunions over and over throughout the year, whether it was for Super Bowl games, special events, BBQs, or simple days to just come over and fellowship together. All of my cousins grew up together and supported one another whenever and wherever we could, like at school games and functions. We were alive and in color.

My grandparents' property was located on the East Side of South Oceanside, and back when land was sold in bulk, my grandfather built his own house, which is how we hosted so many of us. It was big enough to have all of us in the house. It was crowded at times, but it was normal for us.

My parents lived right next door to my grandfather's house, so we were neighbors. When we would go to the house, we would greet whoever was there, then dash to the massive backyard. It was so big; we could go back there and just play for hours and never get bored of all of the things to keep us occupied.

At the top of the hill in his backyard, he built a hoop with a half court that did not have the regulation or official basketball lines like the ones at the park, so we created our own marks for the free throw line and out of bounds by the cracks in the cement. There was no net on the rim to stop the ball from just going anywhere after you made a shot.

When all the family would come over, we played pickup games. We were able to have five-on-five teams made up of several different teams. We argued and competed hard, but we never fought or swung at each other or anything like that. Having so much family around taught me about love, loyalty, and togetherness. I had the best memories of Papa's place.

When I wasn't playing sports, I was also interested in toys and cartoons like other normal kids at that age enjoyed, like Transformers and Voltron. Some of you reading this may have to look these up on the Internet. They were on early in the morning on Saturdays, and my siblings and I all watched them together.

Television was rare to have in those days, so there was only one in the house that we all had to share. We would spend days using our imaginations, playing the roles of all those superhero characters. As the youngest, I always had to be the worst power. Garrett, of course, was always the leader; he was our leader. Letrice was the wonder girl, and Chris got to pick next, so of course, I was last. Here's a good example. With Voltron, I was the yellow lion, the left foot of Voltron...the one who never really saved the day. I was accustomed to being the last choice; I was the youngest of four at the time, so I accepted it.

I had to find something cool, so I adapted my own superpower to compensate for my lack of having a voice. I had all this protection around me, so I was never afraid of saying anything at any time, anywhere, and to anyone. When I did say what I wanted, my whole family would come to my rescue.

While our uncles and aunties got together at the house, the kids would go out to the neighborhood park. We all would play outside near Papa's house up the hill at the community park called Balderrama. The neighborhood was really diverse, with a mixture of cultures; we had Blacks, Hispanics, and Samoans. It was a pretty rough, tough, and poor neighborhood. We had our share of gangs, but my cousins kept me away from that.

I was never really afraid of being jumped or getting involved in gangs because there were so many of my family members in the city. We were a gang by ourselves. There were close to forty or fifty children, and out of them, I am the youngest child of all my cousins as the last-born of that generation from my uncles and aunts.

I was affectionately referred to as the baby cousin, Tray.

I was sometimes able to tag along with my older "cuzzos," as we called ourselves. The rule was as long as

I didn't get them in trouble with my parents by wandering off, I was good.

All they did at the park was go run the basketball courts because they were all super tall. They dominated the court for hours and rarely lost. Plus, they would talk so much trash while embarrassing their opponents. Sometimes, I would go play on the swings and around the park, but most of the time, I would just watch them play. In between the games, I would get up from the sidelines and take the extra basketballs that were on the side of the court. I would dribble and shoot while they were on the other end of the court, but as soon as they came back down the court, I dashed out of the way.

Because I was the baby brother and could just call over my brothers, my sister, and my cousins (my superpowers), I had the feeling I could say whatever I wanted to, and yes, you got it...my mouth got me in trouble a lot.

One day, while playing at the park, I decided to put that power to the test. A kid I hadn't seen before was bullying others on the slides and swings. Perhaps he was new to the neighborhood, but I wasn't a fan of people making me or others feel less than. Like David, my reference in the introduction, I don't like Goliaths making fun of and bullying other kids. In this instance, I wanted to get on the swings, as all the kids did, but when my turn came, he wouldn't let me get on either. He pushed all the kids out of the way when they tried to get on. I was not going to back down, so I challenged him. He was at least twice my size, but I knew I wasn't alone, and I knew my family was playing on the basketball courts some ways off.

It had stormed and rained some days before, so there were huge puddles of mud next to the swings. When it was my turn to try and get on the swings, the boy started to try and bully me off, as he did to the others. But I stood up to the boy, and he pushed me with ease. I pushed him back, but he didn't move much. He responded by pushing me back harder to where I plastered my back to the ground, and he stood over me. Then, to make a statement, he took my shoe off, then slung one of them in the huge puddle of mud. All the kids backed off and left me there on the ground, with my shoe in the mud. Someone immediately ran over to tell my big brother and cousins, but my sister Letrice had already had her eyes on the situation and had seen what had happened, and she was coming over fast with bad intentions. She immediately addressed my adversary. She yelled, "Hey, what are you doing to my little brother?" The boy got into my sister's face, and my sister stepped up to him just like I did a moment earlier. Instead of the confrontation I had where there was pushing and shoving, the boy punched my sister hard, like a boxing jab to the stomach. Letrice just had a look of surprise when he punched her.

Even at this young age, I knew it was taboo for a boy to punch a girl. After the surprised look left my sister's face in half a second, it changed. Her eyes went black, and she was filled with rage. She swung at his face and landed a two, three, and four combination punch like Mike Tyson, and the kid fell to the ground. As he lay there on the ground, Letrice stood over him, began kicking him and stomping on him, and beat him down in front of the entire park. After the beat down, she made him go deep in the mud puddle, retrieve my shoe, hand it to me, and apologize. Then she turned to me and said, "I got you!"

The legend of my sister's toughness became known and legendary in our family and around the blocks. From that point in my mind, she was my protector. It's not that my brothers did not want to, she just took the role in our house as a person who will always stand up for all of us. Family over everything.

CHAPTER 2

PK: The Other Side of the Calling

Attending every Sunday at your local community church is one thing. Being what they call the First Family of the city and church community and the son of a pastor is a whole different part of life. There is a lot of good from this divine calling from everyone who follows God's destiny and purpose, and I found the most important thing from being a PK is that from birth, the seed of God is planted into your spirit even if you do not yet understand His teachings.

Growing up knowing the truth about heaven and hell is a blessing because the Bible says, "Train up a child in the way he should go and when he is old, he will not depart from it" (Proverbs 22:6, KJV).

The struggle with being a PK is the stigma that we should always know better than anyone else what is right and what is wrong. It is a known cliché, and they, whoever they are, would always say we are the worst of kids; we should instantly have wisdom because we are blessed of God that our parents are called by God, so we should basically be perfect.

My father, Clarence Crayton Jr., met my mom, married her, and started their family at the age of nineteen. My parents were both originally born in the South from very small country towns. My father is from Winnfield, LA, and my mother, who picked cotton as a child, is from Yazoo City, MS.

They were born only one state away from each other. Only God could orchestrate their lives to intersect in a whole other state, many miles away from their hometowns.

When they were teenagers, my father moved to Oceanside, CA, and my mother moved to San Diego. My mother attended Lincoln High School and came to an Oceanside High School track meet. My dad was running in the meet there, and while looking in the stands, he saw my mother there with friends. With much swagger, he used his charm to approach my beautiful mother, get her number, if that's what they did back then, and convinced my mom to go out on a date with him.

My mom received a lot of attention because she was very smart and beautiful, but what was always important to her was to have a man who grew up in the church, was into God's purpose, and had a mind set on God's Word. I am thankful for obvious reasons that

Mom agreed to meet up with my dad, and I'm so glad they fell in love. Shortly after they met, they married at the age of nineteen. I say that my mom wanted a different man because, at the time, my father wanted to chase his dream of music as the drummer for a local band called The Road Runners. They were a pretty big deal and had a promising future.

The night before my father and his band were going to sign a major record deal in Hollywood, God visited my father in a dream and warned him in a clear vision in his dream that hell was real. He gave him a vision of the lake of fire...a dream my father woke up from with the choice to either serve God or ignore what he experienced and continue in his own way, for that was the place that would await him. To this day, my dad still states he knew from that vision that he was called for a greater purpose, which was to pastor and shepherd God's people. My father gave his life to Christ that second and began his path toward becoming a servant to God and obedient to His command. He went from running track to playing with The Road Runners to running his race of destiny in the kingdom of God.

This changed a generational legacy for my family.

Church and being in God's service has always been a focal point in my family and is in my life. My family attended the local church in our neighborhood, and as far as I remember, it was what we did. He wasn't the pastor of his own church yet, but he was getting trained and mentored by the best ministers and very prominent people in our community. Everyone could see and hear the gift of the Holy Spirit within him. I have never disliked going to church; it never seemed unfamiliar, as it has always been the way for my life.

My family was not rich at all or even comfortable. My parents worked normal jobs and really worked hard to make ends meet. There were five of us kids that needed to eat and have clothes. They tried their best to give us the best normal environment. I did not grow up privileged in any way. We were not well off as far as financial things back then, but we couldn't tell because family helped family. If we had to stay at my aunt's house, so be it. If we moved around the city, so be it. One thing was for sure: we never went without having food on the table. That was my parents' priority.

In the early year of 1985, my father sat us down as a family and told us kids that we would be leaving our local church to plant a church of our own. My father named the church Faith Temple. We relocated and started in a small startup building that was on the other side of the city, far from the East Side of Oceanside, where we grew up and away from all my friends. This building was in a part of Oceanside called Deep Valley Oceanside.

Deep Valley was one of our toughest neighborhoods. The building my dad rented was smack dab in the middle of that hood. Gangs such as the Deep Valley Bloods, Deep Valley Crips, and the Mesa Mexican gang were all within blocks of each other, but that is where God established us to be.

I remember the first day we opened the doors with seven people in attendance...yes, you guessed it...it was just the family. My father stood in the pulpit and preached his sermons with just us in the audience. We had a full service. We held the doors open while we sang the hymns and praise and worship songs that we practiced with my parents. My siblings and I were the original praise and worship team. Garrett played the saxophone, Letrice played the tambourines, Chris had the maracas, and I had two African sticks. Nikki was too young, so she stayed in the car seat while we all sang songs on stage. We sang one song over and over again called "Star in the Morning."

He urged us to play our instruments and sing so loud that people heard us as they walked past the liquor stores next to us. We followed our parents' lead.

We eventually moved permanently from our home near the East Side into the neighborhood so that my parents could be closer to the church and office. My father had the vision, and he was very committed and determined to obey God's calling upon his life. He wanted to serve, not be served. He wanted to exemplify godly character and moral courage, and he still does to this day. My parents did not have any college degrees, but they were united in building a church that helped others come to know God.

We grew up in a normal parent-led home with rules based on the Word of God. Don't misunderstand, they were strict—not so strict that we couldn't have some fun, but we had biblical rules and principles constantly spoken and taught to us about purpose and living a life for Christ, like do not lie, cheat, steal, etc.

My parents were determined to partner in the common goal of establishing the best family atmosphere and to teach their children how to rely on faith that moves mountains, and with God, nothing is impossible. This was spoken to us over and over, even if we didn't know the real meaning behind what it meant yet. Most importantly we will do this all as a family, all together.

Having parents that were called by God was special. The purpose of love in their heart was extraordinary.

It takes a special anointing and commitment to the call to put your life in front of people while you exemplify faith, character, and obedience, and resisting temptation is not easy in the least.

Most view pastors to be professional salesmen who are not true to their calling, only wanting to get rich off of other people's emotions. Not my parents! Not my father! He was an example of a man with integrity, and we got to witness this every day. My mother ministered that her mission always included making sure we all became great citizens in our local community.

Over a period of several months, people began walking through the doors of Faith Temple. Oceanside has one of the largest military bases in the U.S., and Deep Valley was near the back gate entrance for the Marines to get on base. Young military couples and single men and women who came to Oceanside from all parts of the country started coming in as they settled into the city.

Families were looking for a church home, and the word spread quickly in the neighborhood about our church. My father's preaching style was unique and nontraditional from the hooping and theatrical performances many were used to. He taught like a professor in a classroom and in such a way that others didn't just come for the music to feel good and then go home. He stood in front of the pulpit, spoke without hesitation, and taught the people through practical lessons with real-world applications. His aim was to help people understand how to live by faith, and he explained it in the simplest of tone and form.

He studied this new wave of teaching from others like his mentor, the late Apostle K.C. Price, and the ministerial styles of Kenneth Copeland, among others. My dad watched the lifestyles of those he listened to and allowed himself to be influenced by. He demonstrated that it was about how they lived, not simply about what they said. It had to line up with the Word of God.

The 700 Club and other television ministry programs are something I loved to watch with my mom. She is an amazing example of a super-duper prayer warrior. As they grew mighty in the Word, so did the church. Faith Temple began to grow at a rapid pace from the original seven to more than one hundred people and families.

God was really growing the church. The more my father studied and applied himself, the more people came. The Bible says in Joshua 1:8 (KJV), "This book of the law shall not depart out of thy mouth; but thou shalt meditate therein day and night..."

More people continued to walk through the church doors, and the ministry was being blessed. Many were coming from other states and were away from their families and familiar surroundings, so it was especially important that God be the center of our church.

My parents were visionaries and innovators, and they wanted to grow the congregation, not for their own self-image, but to help families become better and grow stronger. Our church made this happen through ministries that met the needs of those God sent; there was weekly Bible study, children's church, teen ministry, and teachings and classes on marriage and being single. Eventually, Faith Temple would offer courses of higher learning when it received recognition as an accredited biblical college.

Never wanting the shine, their motivation was not to become some big, huge megachurch for the sake of size. My parents were just trying to save as many souls as they could and then teach them the message of the "good news."

In addition to the solid, anointed teaching of the gospel, church was also fun. My father loved the arts, like dancing, performance, and worship, because of his love for music. When my dad gave up the band for the pulpit, God did not take away his love for music; He simply gave him a different purpose for it...to glorify God and edify the people of God.

Before we had a children's church, we would all sit in the back with the other kids and listen to the messages. The congregation was getting larger, and we started a helps ministry of volunteers, which included ushers and others who wanted to serve God.

As an adolescent, I always felt the calling upon my life, but I was young, so I really didn't understand what I wanted to do in church. My brothers and sisters were old enough to be ushers, so that's what they did for service. All I saw were grownups putting their hands in the air and singing to God, so I copied that. We got to participate in the children's choir known as the King's Kids and performed in our annual Christmas and Resurrection (Easter) plays. I got over the fear very early in my life when it came to performing in front of a crowd. I was not afraid to act or sing.

My father was proud of his family, so he would often have us stand and recognize us to the congregation and guests, eliminating the fear of the limelight. My parents did everything, it seemed, to help anyone who came through that door. Strangers were trying to make transitions from difficult situations like divorce or overcoming hard times. Some families even lived with us until they could get on their feet. We gave away things like televisions and clothes. We even shared our rooms with families. God helped us to be true examples of His compassion on the earth, and my parents had plenty of it for the people they led.

We were taught as the pastor's kids that we had a responsibility to set an example of obedience for the other children in the church, so we had to be on our best behavior. It was incredible to see my parents build the ministry from nothing into a successful, thriving church. The church started to really grow; the congregation also began to see the blessings upon their own personal lives. My parents taught me all the good moral characteristics, and I had great siblings as examples, too.

My brother Garrett was a genius. My sister Letrice was a protector. And my brother Chris was my best friend...as we were a year apart. My little sister Nichelle was the baby girl. What I learned in church was to be kind to the poor and love others. Because I constantly saw my parents do this, I would often imitate their behavior at school as well.

I easily made new friends everywhere I went. I didn't go by Tray at the time. That was my nickname at home and to my neighborhood friends, but in elementary schools, I was known as Clarence Crayton III. I always was cool to kids who got picked on or those who felt out of place. Most kids were drawn to me because my personality and my athletic ability would often draw attention to me.

At a young age, I was convinced my purpose from God would include the use of sports to help kids who were being bullied and mistreated or felt like misfits. I felt a sense or need to always protect the students other kids were being cruel to because they weren't considered one of the "cool kids." I would unashamedly speak up for them because I watched my parents stand up for the causes they believed in.

We moved around a lot, living in many different communities from third to sixth grade. I think I went to four different elementary schools in the district, so I made several new friends all over the city. Finally, we settled into a neighborhood that became our home from my sixth-grade year until I graduated from high school.

Getting an education always came first. Homework and classroom studies were a priority from day one. No good grades, no games. My parents instilled in us at an early age the importance of discipline and maintaining a sense of order.

I was always pretty popular in school, so I did run for leadership positions in school, like class treasurer, associated student body president, and school representative, to name a few. Although my dream was to be a professional athlete, my goal was to give back to my family, my parents, and the church. I had a list of things I wanted to accomplish. I wanted to never struggle financially again. I wanted to be rich.

Proverbs 10:22 (KJV) says, "The blessing of the Lord, it maketh rich, and he addeth no sorrow with it." God may not add the sorrow, but life sure does like to stick its two cents in wherever it can!

I wanted to be a sports star who made a difference and gave glory to God for it all. I had dreams of building my father this huge church with the millions of dollars I would earn as a pro in the NFL.

I had it all planned out, or so I thought. I would follow an illustrious football career, and then I would transition to become a radio figure as a Christian psychologist who helped people solve their problems using talk radio as the platform...I had it all figured out.

Habakkuk 2:2 (KJV) states, "And the LORD answered me, and said, Write the vision, and make it plain upon tables, that he may run that readeth it."

I would never let go of that vision. I couldn't if I wanted to. It was as if it were imprinted upon my soul. It was all I ever wanted to do, and with my family as my motivation and main source of support...nothing was going to stop me!

CHAPTER 3

The Crayton Brothers Uniqueness to the Game

We settled into the home that I would eventually grow up in after living in the deepest part of the valley, which was located on top of a hill right above a local school named Pacifica Elementary. Oceanside wasn't known yet for its hotbed of talented, athletic kids, but as the years went by, a lot of us would receive accolades, awards, and scholarships to many types of universities and colleges.

All the kids from the neighborhood would gather together and play every Saturday at this elementary school. More than forty to fifty of us in the neighborhood would come out to either play or watch on the huge playground. It was similar to Balderama Park, which was on the East Side of Oceanside. There were basketball courts, soccer, baseball, and, of course, football fields.

My older brother Garrett was one of the teenagers who would go down there all the time to play with my cousins and his friends every weekend. Garrett, who is six years older than I am, of course, had a different crew than Chris and me because of the age difference, so the kids he played with were out of our league, but we always wanted to play with Garrett's age group.

Chris and I begged Garrett all the time to let us play with the bigger kids, but he would always refuse and tell us, "No." I think he just didn't want us to get hurt because he always let us tag along if we could. Finally, one day, Garrett said yes and agreed to let us play with his friends, but he made it clear there was to be no messing around or crying like a baby. I responded, "We can be tough. Let's go! We can play with the big boys." The thing was, they played tackle football...with no pads.

I was the smallest and skinniest kid on the field, and because of my age and stature, whoever lined up on the opposite side of me cheated to the other players and paid more attention to the other players who often got the ball. So, I told Garrett to throw me the ball as I was wide open the entire game. Garrett was reluctant at first because these guys were hitting and tackling each other hard.

Garrett, who was always the quarterback, said I was finally going to get the ball after we broke one of the huddles. I was like, "Yeah!" He told me just to go ten yards, then turn around, and he would throw me the ball. So, I did just what he told me. Garrett scrambled for a bit, then threw a strike to my chest. I was so wide open there was only one person in front of me. I juked the one big kid and saw nothing but green in front of me, and I thought that was it; I was about to score and show these big kids I arrived. I got real cocky because I was already thinking about what kind of end zone dance I was about to perform, and out of nowhere, from a direction I didn't see, this huge Samoan kid came out of nowhere and knocked me about 5 yards from where he hit me. I literally ate the grass and got the wind knocked out of me for the first time. I felt like I couldn't breathe, and I gasped for air because I had landed on my stomach. Gravity's invisible force introduced my body to the ground while the ball was wedged in between. This was not the kind of airtime anyone looked to get!

Garrett was the first one to run over and check on me, and as he picked me up, while I was still gasping for air, he leaned into my ear and said, "You'd better not start to cry, or you are never coming with me again."

Trying to catch my breath, I wiped my tears, and he let me gain my breath again. The next thing he said was, "See, that wasn't that bad, was it?"

I responded by saying no in agreement when the truth was it was that bad. Garrett taught me a lot of valuable lessons. He continued and said, "Don't you ever let anyone see you do that again!" Meaning I was never to look as if an opponent had got the best of me. I knew what he meant immediately and got up as if the impact was not as painful as it was.

I learned about the toughness of the game at that very moment and that temporary pain comes with the game. I wiped the grass out of my nappy Afro, lined up red-eyed and snot-nosed, and played the next play frustrated, but I gained respect from the older kids.

They got a glimpse of my toughness after taking that hit. They all came up to me after the game and gave me, the little man, respect for not quitting. What Garrett said was true; although I took a big bruise, I felt good after, like I passed and accomplished something through the pain. His last words during a short conversation when we were walking home and his sage advice were, "Keep your head on a swivel; you never think you made it in the end zone until you get in the end zone, understand."

I carried that statement throughout my entire sports career. I never stopped short of any end zone ever again. In fact, I would run an extra 5 yards past the end zone every time I scored from that day forward, just as a reminder to run to the end of the tape. That day was significant; it shaped my heart and etched in my mind that I was going to and willing to put my body on the line for this game. It's not the fanciness of the game but the toughness of competitors, leverage, and grit. I loved the game and its toughness that much, and I wanted to be the toughest. Garrett taught me and Chris how to put our shoulders down and how to absorb the hits from the older kids the right way. Little did I know, this would be advice that not only carried me in the sports world but beyond football, and life was going to teach me to be watchful of my surroundings and to never assume I had made it. I knew I could never let my guard down.

The older kids saw and felt the toughness of the Crayton brothers as we started hitting and tackling. The more we played the game with them, the more our confidence grew, and our skills were honed and sharpened.

We were the epitome of "iron sharpeneth iron" (Proverbs 27:17, KJV). The better one of us got, the other two would always benefit. Our camaraderie and unity made us a force to be reckoned with.

They started picking us to play earlier when the captains were picked, and other peers my age would be the last players picked or not get picked at all, and they had to settle for playing only with the kids my age.

Playing with the older, bigger, faster, and more skilled kids gave me an advantage early, as the game began to slow down for me, and the competition became a tutorial in my advancement as an athlete.

My brother Garrett, who became my other coach besides my dad, saw all the potential and possibilities as my mind and body regarding the game began to progress. I no longer ran away or avoided contact anymore, and I learned how to break tackles and avoid getting hit head-on unless I initiated the contact.

I knew to always practice and play the game at full speed. I had to always give 100 percent or nothing. I got better and better every day. I practiced day and night. I wanted to be great, not mediocre, not lazy or average; those words were never associated with my vocabulary. I didn't fully understand all the talent I had or had tapped into, all that I was capable of as of yet, but I felt the gift of greatness inside of me, and it fueled me to never stop or give up until I attained it. Jeremiah 29:11 reminds me that before I was formed in my mother's womb, God knew me...He knew Tray! He said to me... "I'm God, and I know all, and I see all, and I knew from your father's father's grandfather that eventually you would be born, and you would come out of that lineage. I needed you for such a time as this." And like David, at a young age, I was ready!

POP WARNER

The principles of toughness and working hard were not just implemented as a football player. I also played other recreational sports, including basketball, baseball, and even track, at the Boys and Girls Club, the YMCA, and city youth programs. The path to the dream of playing in the NFL started with the nationally recognized Pop Warner Football League. A lot of pro athletes credit their Pop Warner experiences as the first step in helping them develop the fundamentals of the game.

I anticipated playing in Oceanside Pop Warner (OPW) for years. My brother, cousins, and the older kids on the playground all played. The legal age to become eligible to play was seven. On top of starting his church, my dad was big on playing sports because of the discipline, mental toughness, and teamwork gained from it and the "we, not me" attitude that he knew sports would instill in us. Oceanside Pop Warner was known for having great teams around San Diego County, and we were in North County.

Saturdays were an all-day affair for families, and the games started very early, beginning at 6 a.m. and going strong until 5 p.m. People had lawn chairs and tents in preparation to watch all of the divisions play. It was an all-day event, even if their child's team game was over, because others supported the youth from the city. The community support for OPW was serious and diehard. The strong bond among the teams would play a huge part in getting us prepared to carry the tradition from little league to playing at the local high school level and from there to compete for C.I.F. championships and bring the trophy to our city.

My brother Chris got to play one year ahead of me, of course, so I had to wait a whole year, anticipating and anxiously waiting for my turn to put on the helmet and pads. Garrett was, without a doubt, our role model when it came to sports because he was so good at every sport he played. He was an excellent basketball player and would later receive a basketball scholarship as a point guard after high school. He played the quarterback position in football, which, as you learned earlier, is why I developed a passion for the position. He demonstrated to me what the position was all about and why it was the most important position on the field. His leadership and the sense of responsibility as the QB was impressive. Not to mention, the QB got to touch the ball on every play. I wanted that.

In those days, Black QBs were rare, and Garrett was a huge San Diego Sports fan. His favorite player at the time was Dan Fouts. He wore the number fourteen and played that position because of him. He was inspirational in the way that he wasn't afraid to break the barrier of becoming a Black quarterback for any division, whether Pop Warner, high school, college, or the NFL, and I wanted to be just like him.

Sign-up day for Oceanside Pop Warner had finally come. First, Garrett always told us, "Your number should mean something to you, even if it was just because it was your favorite player's number." I knew exactly what number I wanted to be, and when numbers are assigned, or they let you pick numbers, the best players always get to pick first. For me, my choice was the number seven!

It was my choice for several reasons. First, because in biblical numerology, it is God's number of completion. Second, there were seven members of our family. And third, it was half of Garrett's number and a single digit.

Chris and I were only fourteen months apart and inseparable. Everywhere he went, I went, and we were fortunate to play on the same team a lot on the playground and when we played on official teams. We got to play on the same team in Pop Warner often. We were known as the Crayton Brothers!

Usually, in the first year of playing football, you get adjusted to hitting and tackling with a helmet, shoulder pads, and all the equipment. However, because I played tackle football with Garrett and the other bigger kids, I was not afraid of the contact. I just needed to get used to moving around in the gear and seeing the field through a helmet.

God gifted me with the abilities and talents to run, catch, and use my quick instincts, so it was easy for me to adjust. I had no fear when it came to tackling. I actually felt more protected, having played so much tackle football without the equipment. I felt like I was already built tough.

My father coached our Pop Warner teams as an assistant, and he knew his boys had something different, but it was time for others to take notice. After practice, many parents came up to us to tell my dad the Crayton brothers were special. As crazy good as I was my first year, Chris was better. He was faster than me and a serious playmaker. I loved everything about my first year, and I loved to go to practice. We were a decent team my first year, mostly made up of kids playing an organized game in pads. It was complete with real referees; the field had lines marked for out-of-bounds and the line of scrimmage, not to mention the penalties. This was the real deal according to the real rules of the game in the real atmosphere. We were okay in my first year, and I finally got the taste of a full season.

The second year came quickly; we all moved up from the mighty mite division to the Jr. Pee Wee. The bigger the division, the more experienced the competition. Players were returning for their second- or third-year terms.

There were some first-year players, but most of us were all a year older, now eight and nine, and our minds and bodies now knew what to expect. The first year, Chris and I were both running backs. That was the glamor position for the best athlete who played running back at that age because they got the ball every play. Kids who played QB just handed the ball off, mostly because it was harder to throw the regulation ball at that age. I wanted the ball in my hands all the time so I could score touchdowns, so that is the position I played.

Chris and I played so well together that first year. I was the rookie, and Chris, a bit more seasoned, got a lot more carries the first year, and that fueled me to be better as a second-year player. My second year at Pop Warner was a defining moment in my young football career as we started to share the load.

Oceanside Pop Warner had so many talented players on each team. Many were phenomenal athletes. It was so hard to make it to the next level that a lot of our dreams stopped at the high school level. I was able to play with and watch many great athletes that started in Pop Warner over the years. One being an all-time great and a future NFL Hall of Famer, Junior Seau.

I got to spend a lot of time with him because Garrett and Junior were really good friends and teammates growing up. They hung out and played regularly, and since Junior had a younger brother my age, we, too, played together when our big brothers got together.

Eventually, I got to know all the Samoan kids in the community, and since there was a Samoan church that moved into a building right next door to my father's church, we played and got really close to their community, as they are big on family culture and togetherness. They are great athletes, big, fast, and talented, much like I had grown up seeing in the Black community on the East Side. The teams I played on were well-diversified, consisting of a mixture of Samoans, Blacks, Mexicans, and Whites. Oceanside, at that time, was by no means a rich place to live; it was a beach town lined with palm trees and boasting one of the most beautiful harbors in California. It was not like other places in California, and adding the melting pot of people because of the Marine Corps base, it was like a melting pot of diversity. Exposure to this mixture of cultures would prove beneficial and integral to my future.

In year two, we had a Mexican coach named Richard "Coach" Badillio. To this day, he was one of the best head coaches I ever had. The staff he put together was amazing, and it included my dad. My dad was still putting in God's work and building his church and made the time to coach me and my brother Chris. My dad was so instrumental, being there in the beginning, laying the foundation of our football careers. As an adult, understanding his sacrifices of time and energy and maintaining the household responsibilities, too, serves me so well.

My parents were not well off financially, and the fees to play were upward of $200.00–$300.00 per player. But my parents, with all their support, made it work because they wanted us all to participate in what we wanted to do, and I wanted nothing more than to play Pop

Warner. They preached and stood on faith and that God would supply all of our needs and give us the desires of our hearts. I may not have known exactly how God did it; I just know that He did it, and the faith of my parents invited in God's provisions for us to participate in the things that seemed unobtainable at times.

I know what they sacrificed so that I could play. Later on, I found out Coach Badillio also wanted the Crayton brothers on his team, and he made sure he helped us secure scholarships offered by OPW, and we were very grateful.

Coach Badillio told my father about a new offensive scheme that would tailor a way to have Chris and me showcase our skills equally on the field at the same time. He introduced a rare offensive concept called the single wing. This was what they now call the wildcat formation. Yes, in 1985, our coach innovated and ran this system without the traditional QB under the center. It is used a lot in schemes today on all levels.

It was a shotgun-type formation that used a direct snap of the ball straight to the running back (Chris one play, me the next), squatting five yards from the center with a fullback to the right or left of us, depending on the side we would run to. That took practice and skill, not just for us but our center and lineman.

We ran dive sweeps, counters, and fullback dives, and it was something other teams had never seen before. Not only did we have this new dynamic offense that featured our speed, but we also had a tough-nosed, fearless, stingy bunch of kids who loved to hit and play defense.

As players, we compared the stick marks (the other team's color helmet) on our helmets, since ours were white, to see who got the biggest hits. The more you had, the tougher you were.

This new, unstoppable offense of kids who knew how to tackle and knew the fundamentals made us special, and we experienced one of the all-time best seasons for a team in Oceanside Pop Warner history.

We were so unstoppable that we began to make the city news with garnered state exposure. I would compare it to a Little League team getting the chance to represent their city and state region in Omaha for the Little League World Series title. The news in our community spread fast, and the entire city of Oceanside began to support and show strength in numbers at our games. The entire community was behind us.

Our team, the Oceanside Tigers, broke several Pop Warner records. Our practices were professionally conducted, and the coaches were in unison in all phases of the game. We had intense fundamental hitting drills every practice. Our coaches preached discipline, a desire to win, togetherness, brotherhood, teamwork, competition, and what perfection means.

We competed hard against each other every day because we wanted to have the perfect season (no losses).

My father put in the extra work with us as he showed us the fundamentals of carrying the ball as we watched the greats like Walter Payton and Eric Dickerson during televised pro games. My dad would observe players and drill us on the fantastic plays we would witness. He'd ask us, "See how he cut back, see how he read the hole?"

The new system had the Crayton brothers shining like stars. Chris and I would always keep and compare our stats to see who played the best in any given game. Chris would run for 140 yards, get three touchdowns, and return punts. And in that same game, I tried to match him by running 120 yards, getting two touchdowns, and returning kickoffs.

We would flip-flop games, but Chris would usually get the most touchdowns, and I might get the most yards.

Normally, our age group played early in the morning, but due to the attention from the support of the city, we were invited many times to play several games in front of great crowds under the lights at the high school stadium.

At this young age, we knew what we were playing for—greatness and the team goal of finishing the perfect season. We relished the glow of the lights and screams from the crowd like we were high school superstars.

In the ninth game of the season, we made the invitation to play in the state championship game; then, it would be the West Coast Regional semifinals, one game away from the National Championship Pop Warner Super Bowl invitational held in Florida. We played a team called South Coast, which I believe was in the Orange County area, for the rights to host the finals.

It was the first time in Oceanside Pop Warner history that a team made it this far. Young eight- and nine-year-old kids were getting the experience of big-time football. The local newspaper and the number one reporter for the *North County Times* covered the story of our team, encouraging the city to come watch these special groups of kids trying to achieve something special for the city of Oceanside.

We did not disappoint, winning in convincing style with a score of fifty-five to zero. The following day after the game, we never missed church, sore and all. A member came and brought the newspaper in, and for the first time ever, I was on the cover of the sporting page. A huge, larger-than-life picture of me in my number seven jersey making a cutback run for a 55-yard touchdown, and the bottom caption said: "Tray Crayton ran for 105 yards and a touchdown after beating the South Coast football team!"

My first taste of stardom! I still have that clipping from 1985. It made me famous among the kids at school, and it was a great feeling.

The stage was set, and our dream was right in front of us, hosting the city's first-ever regional final game in our home city of Oceanside against Yuma Arizona Pop Warner, the number one team versus the number two.

I'll skip the anticipation and just mention we lost that game two to zero on a safety. I got tackled in the end zone for safety. In the single-wing shotgun formation and upon the snap, the hole was clogged, and I had nowhere to go. I fought my hardest to get out of the end zone but eventually got tackled, and although it happened really early in the game, it was the defining score of the game. We fought hard for that game but lost on that one play. Our team was devastated, being so close to becoming the National Pop Warner Super Bowl Champions. That was the first time I was brokenhearted from the game of football, and I never wanted to lose in a championship game again. I vowed never to lose a championship game, and it was important for me to become a champion. From that point, I didn't want to lose again on or off the field.

Section 2: Getting Prepared for the Show

"I am the greatest. I said that even before I knew I was."

—Cassius Clay

CHAPTER 4

Make Your Own Stardom

The bond from that team still resonates with me, and I often reminisce about the pure love that team shared. It really did shape the foundation that we each carried into our high school careers. That season was also the last time I played the running back position.

The next year, I didn't have Coach Badillio anymore, and being a year older, I switched my position to quarterback, as I was ready to take on a more prominent role as a leader of the team.

My father could no longer coach us on the sidelines as the church began to grow, and his responsibility to the ministry grew along with it. But he never stopped coaching us from the sidelines and still attended all my games.

For the next four Pop Warner seasons, I worked on honing my skills so that I could follow in Garrett's footsteps and become a quarterback in high school.

I knew that I wouldn't be running the ball as much, but as I began to study more football and watching the NFL, I wanted to be something. I wanted the ball in my hands and the respect of my teammates, and the quarter back is that type of position. Since Garrett groomed me early about the QB position and prepared my mind for the highs and the lows, I was fearless and unafraid to take on the responsibility of winning or losing.

I was okay with having that put on my shoulders. For one, that is what I learned in church that Jesus Christ did for us, so what better way to honor Him with this gift?

As a little kid, in my young mind, somehow, this was something I understood and embraced. It's what the position of captain and the leader of a team was all about.

I worked and practiced very hard. I pushed and pushed, and my summers were dedicated to the dream within me; I knew with the hard work ethic I could grow my skill level to help me become elite. If I put the work in, gave it my all, extended and pushed myself beyond the limits, God would tell me this in my gut: "What you think you can't do, you can do!" I worked with my dad on the track (one of his areas of expertise) to build my endurance to become faster. While other kids were playing in the streets, I was running hills and valleys—Oceanside was full of both—trying to get better.

The bonus was these times of training, coaching, and drilling principles into me were also special and appreciated times alone with my dad. This must be how God feels when He is leading, guiding, and directing our steps. God desires one-on-one, intimate moments with us, not just when we succeed and give our "thank you" speeches when we've won the prize or trophy, but even more during the process of the journey.

Each year, I took the initiative to try and get better; I practiced throwing the ball up in the air to myself, too, throwing it through tires or whatever drills I could learn or make up.

My brothers always made time to take me to a park or some other place in Oceanside where someone was playing ball, whether football or basketball, to work on my skills.

I wanted to put the Crayton name that my grandfather built in front of millions of people. My parents had established a name associated with character, integrity, grit, and responsibility, and it is an outstanding name, so I wanted to add to this legacy in my own way.

We all had our ambitions of trying to make it to the pros, but out of all of my twenty or so gifted and talented cousins who were in the Oceanside area, none of them had been given a shot at a big-time scholarship offer.

I was determined to break that cycle. Throughout my elementary and middle school years as an athlete, all I did was win city and county championships in basketball and most other sports.

In our household, we judged our success by the trophies we received, and I was way behind. Anything I did when it came to sports, I wanted to be number one.

I pushed myself every day in order to get better and better, and although I had the God-given abilities to play sports, I knew that just off my pure talent wasn't going to be able to be the best I had to work hard and train harder than my opponents, so I visualized and pushed myself against invisible oppositions, and that thrived me to get better, rather it be in practice, after practice, or on my own spare time. At this young age, I had the drive and the fortitude to understand that in order to be the best, I must not rest simply on talent alone.

I had the mindset that no matter how many victories or trophies I had, I could never rest on them and think that I had arrived.

As I became more and more comfortable with my new role as a leader and a QB, I began to focus on how my church life and upbringing and my participation in sports were influencing one another and were parallel in many ways.

Just like I didn't play around with God and the institution of the church, I didn't play about sports. My parents were hard workers and preached both in word and deed good moral character and the importance of education so that we did not have to suffer from not having the things they desired later in life.

Garrett, although he was a great athlete in his own right, hit the books hard and was a straight-A student. He pushed himself and was a big example for all of us about being serious in the classroom and our academics. He paved a passable road and mapped out for us a strategy that would lead us to achieve greatness in the classroom as well as on the field. He lived it out before us, becoming the ASB president and other areas of being a representative when it came to school achievements. He was very popular among his friends and showed us that being smart was far better than just being cool. I believed he wanted to be the first Black president. My family would have dinners and would sit at the table and discuss our goals in life, getting out there to try new things and stretch beyond being the typical jock.

My parents pushed us to be in front of the crowds early, so we were not afraid to act, sing, or play in front of crowds. I wasn't too scared to try and run for president of the school and things like that. I went to seek out opportunities for responsible roles at school. I was always popular at school, and I won a lot of the student body elections.

I loved to act and draw. That was my hobby and safe haven beyond sports. I actually played a lot of roles at a young age. One of my favorite memories is playing Danny Zuko in a school play in the sixth grade. At first, I really didn't want to do it because I had a little stage fright, because I felt like the guys at school would laugh at me. But I really liked this girl who was going to be in the female leading role, and she asked me to do it. But when I agreed, I was not aware it was a singing character.

I learned the lines and really worked hard. I had to perform three times in front of the K–3 and the 3–6, and I crushed it! My sister Nikki was in the first grade at the time, and after my performance, she was so proud to call me her brother.

I received flowers for my performance and was just so proud that I didn't care what my friends thought because I had just given the performance of a lifetime!

My parents didn't get to see the show, and I know up until this very day, my mom feels bad for not getting to the performance. She missed it because it was during her work hours. The other moms bragged to her about what a great job I did. This might be irrelevant to most, but it changed me. I felt accomplished and with a sense of pride that I had overcome fear and that my family was proud of me, and I elected to forgo what others thought and would make fun of me for.

I realized that standing in front of the congregation at church worshiping God and the example from my parents made it a lot easier to do things like that. A few weeks later, after that school performance, I went to sixth-grade camp. The camp instructor asked us to go around and introduce ourselves, and for the first time, I said, "Hi, my name is Tray." My teacher attempted to correct me and stated, "It's Clarence." But I advised her that I identified as Clarence only at school, but among my friends and my family, I go by "Tray." And from that camp forward to when I got back to school, my teachers began to call me Tray.

Clarence Crayton III was now "Tray" Crayton and that name was in full force, full-time.

In seventh and eighth grades, I continued to grow in popularity both at school and in the Oceanside community. My friends and I would hang out at bonfires at the beach, the mall, and other places where the older high school teenagers would frequently be. Everywhere we went, they didn't know who my friends were, but all the cool kids knew me and my family, so they would come to show me a lot of respect, and I loved that attention.

I can recall in middle school, we took a trip to Oceanside High School for a luau, a Samoan celebration of song and dance. Junior Seau was not just the best athlete in the state but was one of the most sought-after athletes in the country. Garrett went to the rival high school, but they kept in touch. Everyone knew Junior. He was in the local paper all the time.

The gymnasium was packed with all the elementary students in the district. I didn't tell my friends that he and my brother Garrett were great friends and that they still kept in touch. At the end of the performance, I yelled out, "Hey, Junior!" He turned around because he recognized my voice, and when he saw me, he walked out of his way through the entire assembly of students and stood like a giant in front of my class. He greeted us with a hello and then came straight to me, and we chatted for a quick second. Junior was famous in our community because of his athletic abilities, and that week, he had just committed to play football at the University of Southern California, most famously known as USC.

I got so much school cred from that that it put me at the top of the list at school.

My last year of Pop Warner was when the HS coaches back then used to scout and see who the upcoming stars were. They would pitch to the parents about having their kids play for them and come to their high school athletic program.

Every high school coach in the area approached my parents about me playing football for them, but there was no doubt that I was going to one school and one school only...it had to be El Camino High School.

School and education were always top priority. I knew in order to go to a big university, I had to pass my classes and the SAT. Garrett warned me about that and constantly reminded me that if I wanted to reach the levels like Junior did and play pro football, I'd have to go to class and take school seriously.

My parents made me a promise that if I got good grades in my last year of middle school, I could pick which school I wanted to go to. I achieved a 3.5 GPA, and I was set to start my freshman year at El Camino High School (ECHS). I could be whatever I wanted to be, and I was on my way to seeing the vision that was written on my heart come to pass.

CHAPTER 5

The Freshman Phenom a Heart Conditioned

MY HIGH SCHOOL YEARS

I was a freshman, and there were very few examples of Black QBs in the league that I could emulate in the 1980s and '90s. There was Warren Moon and Doug Williams, for example.

However, in college football, there were many black QBs, but they were used in a specific offensive system known as the triple option.

When it came to drafting QBs to the NFL, they had a specific prototype; players had to be above six feet, be a pocket passer, and were mostly White. There was one QB, however, who was a trendsetter and helped change the perception of having a running and scrambling type of playmaker at the QB position. His name is Randall Cunningham, and he was a game-changer. His impact on the game as a player showed young Black athletes that we can play QB at the NFL level. He demonstrated the ability to be a QB who could throw, run, and scramble to make improvisational plays. Seeing him play for the Philadelphia Eagles grew my confidence that I could do what he is doing and put in my own stamp at the position.

I simulated my game around all that I had on the inside of me, along with what I saw Randall Cunningham do.

My Pop Warner teammates, whom I played with for six years, had to decide which high school city team they wanted to play for: the Green and White, being Oceanside High School, or the Brown and Gold of El Camino High School. It also did depend upon where you lived in the city, too, but there were ways to get a transfer to the school, so you did have a choice of what high school you wanted to attend at that time.

El Camino High School had established a legendary program and had a legendary high school football coach.

The city was constantly growing due to the military base, and due to the lure of the sunshine and the beach, many began to flock to our then-small town. So, although Oceanside High School was the long-time high school of the city, El Camino was the new high school that was established for our growing city.

Garrett and my other family members before me engraved our family name into the fabric of El Camino High.

Garrett played QB, then my cousin replaced him when he left, and after that my other cousin replaced him. So, Friday Night Lights was a recurring mainstay of the Crayton household as well as the extended family.

I got to watch them all play the QB position at El Camino for years. It basically became a tradition for at least one of us to play QB at El Camino, and we were awesome athletes who ran the option scheme.

El Camino was one of the best high school programs, not only in the county of San Diego but in the state for our division. The championship history before I started my freshman season included C.I.F. titles in '76, '82, '84, and '89.

Unfortunately for Garrett and all my cousins that played, their team made it past the second round of the playoffs, but never made it to the finals. The finals were held annually at Jack Murphy Stadium before it was changed to Qualcomm Stadium, the home of the San Diego Chargers. It was Garrett's goal to get a shot at playing in the pro stadium and bringing our city and school a championship.

I was ready for my freshman season. I worked really hard again during the off-season so that I made sure I made the roster of the freshman football team. Although I knew I should be a shoo-in, I didn't ever count on things being handed to me.

El Camino's sports and athletic department was top-notch, but the football program was the heart and soul of our school's athletic tradition. As a freshman, you were not automatically put on a team; you were not entitled to be on the team; you didn't pay to get on a team any more like Pop Warner. You had to earn your way on the team. We had tryouts because we had so many kids wanting to play for the program. One easy way to eliminate the serious players and athletes was not by running drills based on one's catching, running, balance, or agility; rather, your place was sealed by how much heart, desire, and sheer will you had demonstrated. They tested all of this through "Hell Week." What is Hell Week?

Hell Week is the name for practices that are held two times per day for two weeks. It's part of the end of the summer camp schedule and traditionally starts the high school football season for all football programs.

They are significantly harder practices than at any point in the season and are designed to help players with conditioning. It is scheduled in the heat of August to put players through rigorous training to see what shape they are in and if they are prepared for the season.

It originated from actual Marine Corps training programs, and they are all run differently depending on your coach's approach. It is not for punishment, but it is to separate those who prepared themselves for the football season from those who may have need for more training. In Hell Week, there is nothing but hitting and tackling, a sort of initiation, if you will, for any incoming high school football player to see how they measure up. Were you tough enough physically, mentally, and emotionally and also equipped for the sport? I am reminded of the words of Paul in 1 Corinthians 9:27 (NIV), "No, I strike a blow to my body and make it my slave so that after I have preached to others, I myself will not be disqualified for the prize."

We had to push our physical and mental limits; we had to do more than just talk about it (the field was my pulpit); we had to be about it! I had to live the disciplined life I was taught and embraced.

The true victory for the team and coaching is how these brutal two weeks united the team together because of all the hard work we had to do together. I was ready! I was ready from the moment I took to that high school track that day when I was two. Mentally, I was ready because all I ever heard growing up was that I was destined for greatness and would be able to do whatever I set my mind to. So, my mindset and focus were on becoming a QB and being the best. My body followed my mind, and I worked hard at making it a well-oiled machine.

Oftentimes, when there is a tough game or a desperate attempt to overcome something in the season, the team would reference the experience of when we helped push one another's limits, stuck together, and finished the tasks at hand. We would remind each other of how we made it through that period of preparation and in those moments when we needed to dig in, and we needed each other most. This was something I also learned growing up with the most important team ever...family! It was in the times when our close-knit family of multiple generations would come together that I developed a keen sense of unity and synchronization and received the best form of group therapy there is, and it was my goal to pass that example on to my teammates.

I watched Garrett go through his four seasons and Chris's single season. I didn't see what they actually went through physically on the field, as these two weeks are closed to the public. However, I did see how physically worn out they were, and all they did was sleep when they got home and mentally prepared themselves for the next day.

To get ready for my first season, Garrett trained me by designing an off-season program for the year on how to survive Hell Week. It was a pretty simple "get yourself in shape" before the season started. This would be my blueprint with my first off-season program; I ran three to five miles a day per week, with Sunday being my off day. I began running at ten and increased to twenty 100-yard sprints on several hills three days a week for the pleasure of it. On Fridays and Saturdays, we ran pickup basketball games for three to five hours.

After I finished running, he tested my mind. I then completed the fundamentals of throwing and footwork drills. Learning how to throw accurate passes, especially when my mechanics would be physically and mentally challenged, I had to stay focused on my technique.

I did this over and over and over again until I got it right. As a result, I got stronger. This was critical because I was a very skinny athlete. My body was an entire stick man. It was just in our genes. My outside appearance was skinny, but my work on the fundamentals and overall training made my muscles strong. I would do rollout drills and throw every ball imaginable to my brothers. Every drill was full-speed throwing while going out of bounds, tight windows, and when to set my feet and hold the ball to my ear to throw fast and accurately.

I wanted to win at all costs, but I also wanted to establish a reputation for having a dependable and reliable work ethic of leadership on my teams. That meant I always wanted to lead by example.

After successfully making it through Hell Week and the first roster cut of my career, I earned the starting QB position and was also voted team captain...the honor I always wanted to carry. I wanted to be the face and representation of my team; I wanted to be up close and personal; I wanted to be the captain and spokesperson to call the coin toss. And that is exactly what happened.

We went undefeated my freshman year; I had an outstanding debut season. I also started and went undefeated with our freshman basketball team as well. I was enrolled in college prep courses and our ASB program, and I was on track to that D1 offer that I coveted.

Our varsity program won back-to-back C.I.F. titles. We were returning the entire team, and we had some serious Division 1 talent. For the first time in our school history, we were expecting to be three-peat champions and ranked number one in the state in football. Our off-season programs consisted of playing in the county and state's best invitationals.

There was a passing league tournament that was held in Stockton, CA, where we used all the wide receivers, running backs, quarterbacks, and tight ends on offense against the opponents' defensive backs and linebackers. The defensive backs and linebackers are involved, but the center only snaps on the game.

These scrimmages are held at the beginning of summer, right before we take a break to enter fall camp. All the teams participate in scheduled scrimmages, and then there are also the big tournaments where the entire county comes together to play other schools. These games are played without pads, so it is just the schools' practicing shorts and jerseys. It is also a chance to see the best in the county and among the state players.

All the top teams in the state would meet. Our varsity head coach invited me as a freshman, an honor that was rare. I got the opportunity to travel along with the varsity-level players.

I believe our coach was preparing me for the competition. The returning QB was a starter for the past two championships, so I knew that I was not going to be the starting varsity QB, but I was just supposed to tag along.

That QB was very instrumental in my development. The way he ran the team gave me a glimpse of how you, as the QB, are the heart and soul of a team. He knew that I would be his replacement after he graduated that year, and he took me under his wing and taught me the plays and footwork. I was blessed to be in a position where God showed me the favor of having a player want to teach me as a backup and not worry about me outshining them.

We played all the best teams in the state in that tournament. I hadn't ever got into a game when we blew teams out. In one particular game in the tournament, Coach called me into the game as all the upperclassmen got in, and it was such a lopsided score that everyone was going to get a chance to play. I thought this would be my first pass on the varsity level. Instead, Coach called a run play (the triple option) because it was the safest way to ensure the unwritten rule of respect for the game. The play was called the twenty-nine veer option, designed to go to the left. Before we called the play in the huddle, Coach said, "Keep the ball from the fake to the fullback," so I faked the ball to the fullback and took off around the corner. There it was: a wide-open field again. As I cut back into some open green grass, it instantly reminded me of my first catch when I was cocky and didn't look around for the other team or a player who would converge on me. I honed in on my past experience, used my peripheral vision, and saw that my running back was in what we call a pitch relationship, which is when, during the option, even if I am ten or fifteen yards downfield, he stays slightly behind me just in case I need to still pitch it. I juked about three different guys, and then I busted open to the sideline, knowing that the RB was there. Then, at the last second, I pitched it, and the RB scored. I was on cloud nine!

The varsity players all ran over to me and, as they were celebrating, began yelling to the other side, "He's only a freshman!"

SOPHOMORE SENSATION

My off-season program was even more intense when it came to getting bigger, faster, stronger. I was never the one to gain weight, but I did take weightlifting very seriously. I would rest during track season, because I knew already that my body needed to survive through the long football and basketball seasons. When it came to school, I always went to summer school to get ahead and ensure graduation because I had a plan to not have classes my last semester in high school.

I knew going into the season that our freshman team was all revved up to repeat an undefeated season, and because of the talent on varsity, it was hard to jump straight to that level. We had some guys who couldn't play varsity come down to our team as juniors, and that just made us even more dominant. We put our heart and soul into preparing for every game, and we had the mental fortitude and team spirit with a will and resolve to do whatever it would take to win, so we breezed through the league undefeated again. Two straight seasons in the books and two straight championship seasons.

When the JV season ended, the varsity playoffs began, and many high school teams brought up their best sophomore players to participate in practice, travel, and dress out in the games. We don't really play unless there is a huge blowout, as they would mostly use the players who wouldn't normally get the opportunity to participate in varsity games.

We were pretty much the last on the totem pole when it came to getting in a varsity playoff game. In our first playoff game as the two-time defending champions, we were beating our opponent fifty to zero, so with about three minutes left in the game, all the other QBs got called in.

Coach called me to run the last play, and it would be the same option that I ran in the seven-on-seven passing league tournament, but this time, it was for real, in a real game, with pads.

Again, the twenty-seven veer option. I did the exact same thing: I faked it to the fullback and took off around the corner, but this time, I ran the play and took off for about fifty yards, getting tackled at the ten-yard line as the guys were a lot faster at this level.

My parents and the entire school were in the stands, and hearing my name over the stadium speakers on a Friday night game was priceless. The goosebumps I felt gave me a euphoria that I longed to feel.

I got a surprise the following playoff game that I was going to make my first varsity start, not as a QB but as a DB. My entire life, this was one of my goals: to play as a sophomore on varsity and be a three-year letter winner because that was uncommon...and so were my skills. But since I played JV behind our starter, I would rather start than sit on the bench and develop my game.

Our playoff game was against our crosstown rival, Oceanside High. Their QB was one of my next-door neighbors who was my teammate on that 1985 championship Pop Warner team.

We would always talk when we saw each other on the block, but not during rivalry week. This one was for a chance at the semifinals, so losing was not an option. They ran their new up-and-coming "run and shoot" offense with five wide receivers. Our DB coach came up to me and said, "You're starting on defense as the nickel cornerback." This was a great opportunity because I would be sharing the field with our secondary, who was one of the best, not just in our state, but in the country, along with two All-American corners that eventually went top ten in the '97 NFL draft. We also had a four-star, all-state senior linebacker who would sign with UCLA.

Coming out of the locker room and down our stadium stairs, which was the tradition at our school when we took the field, was a lot different this time. I was about to play in a game that would continue our quest for an unprecedented title. Was I nervous? Yes, but I knew I was ready and had built my body and mind for this. In short, we won that game sixty-three to twenty-seven, which included me getting an interception.

I felt like one of the varsity players then and had the respect of the upperclassmen, the trust of the coaches, and the confidence in myself that I could play at that level. The following week, after my first varsity start, to my surprise, Coach moved me up on the depth chart and I had become the second-string to back up our starting QB. In two weeks of getting moved up, I played in both playoff games and started in one. Everything was coming together faster than I thought it would.

In our final game, before we competed for the championship, I would get another test as well. In the semifinal game, our QB, who was the leader of our two-year championship run, got injured, and I had to immediately grab my helmet. I was thrown into the thick of our semifinal game, but this was not like before at the end during a blowout. This was in the middle of the game, with us leading only with a score of seven to zero.

I ran into the huddle, saying, "OMG, this is crazy!" The upper-class lineman, in response, said to me, "Take a deep breath and let's go. You can do this, Tray." I called the play and ran it confidently. Our starting QB was going to be okay and came back in the game after that one play I ran. As the starting QB ran back on the field, and I was running off, we passed a high five to one another and I received deafening applause and cheer from the crowd. All I did was hand the ball off to the running back, but because I got a taste of being in the huddle and directing the offense, I knew I was prepared to play under pressure.

We won that game as well and went on to play in the championship. I became a C.I.F. and state champion that year. I didn't get into the championship game, but I felt that I got the real opportunity to have a taste of what was to come in the years ahead.

The QB I backed up came over to me and said, "Hey, this team is yours now," and sort of passed down the torch to me. I learned so much from observing him. I want to give him credit for being the EC QB I was ready to become.

I thought my chances like that would probably be few and far between, starting the year on JV, but I was proud, and I earned my first ring when we had made history by being the first three-peat in the county and delivering our school's first state championship.

I was awarded a varsity letter and an honorary mention for All C.I.F. after just three games of playing in the varsity playoffs, which checked a goal of mine.

At this point, things began to take off with recruiting.

In my sophomore year, I received the biggest news from my coach: I had my first recruitment letter from Clemson University...a letter I still have framed to this day.

JUNIOR YEAR
Dreaming Big

In my junior year, I became the full-time starter, and I was handed the keys to lead our team full of Ferraris. We came into the season with higher accolades and higher expectations to carry on the winning ways of the program. Again, we were preseason ranked number one in the state and nationally ranked for the first time in our school's history. We returned a lot of our top players from the championship team, plus two of the top twenty-five players in the country.

All the recruiters from every school in the country, from the likes of USC, Michigan, Texas, and all the major conferences, came to our high school in the off-season to watch, film, and evaluate us at our practices. I remember before my first varsity start, and the day before the game, my mom came up to my room, sat on my bed, and said, "I can't believe you are about to be the starting QB for the defending state champions. I am proud that you have worked this hard, Tray. Go get your dream!" That drove me because I always love to make my family proud. I wanted to put my stamp on that entire season, so I had a great junior year, leading the team to another league championship, and we made it back to the finals for a fourth year in a row.

Unfortunately, the outcome of the championship game was not like the years past. Our quest for the four-peat and back-to-back state champions fell incomplete. We lost in the finals, and this was the first time I lost in a championship game since the Pop Warner loss.

I cried because I wanted so badly to win back-to-back state titles, have a four-peat record, and cement my legacy. Although we continued to make it to the championship game, I discovered the outcome is not always guaranteed.

For my performance throughout the season, I won several county and state awards, like being named in the top one hundred underclassmen in the state and best underclassmen to watch, and that catapulted my recruitment after the season. But the one I desired more would be the catalyst that pushed me and fueled me on a deeper level for what would be my last season.

THE SENIOR SEASON
The Courage Chronicles

Before my senior season, many things began to change. My mailbox started to fill up, and I began to get a lot of attention from the big-time football institutions. I was getting letters from the best schools all over the country. I was in preseason national sports magazines; I was being called to do photo shoots with other top players in the state from northern and southern California. It was coming so fast that my name was being mentioned as one of the top football players in the entire country.

I set a goal for myself that I wanted to become an All-American while in high school. Our school had a few that reached this level of elite football status, and that was a personal goal of mine.

There was a tradition at our school that when anyone received such recognition, you gave them a copy of the All-American certificate, and it would be hung up in our school's weight room along with the team picture of the past champions. It was sort of our tribute to immortal legends.

The most popular motivation for earning the All-American title was that they would retire your number. Getting your jersey retired is the biggest honor in sports, no matter what sport a player participates in. I remember telling my parents after we started to see some interest after my sophomore year. I was beginning to get recruited, and at that time, the NCAA could not contact athletes who were becoming upcoming seniors by way of telephone until July of their senior season. The only way of contact during the junior season was through letters in the mail. I would get ten to twenty letters in my mailbox per day from schools soliciting me to come play for their program and represent their university.

The first day that I could receive contact by telephone from school had come, but that first day of contact fell on a Sunday, and no matter what, we were at church. So I had to wait until we got home from church. Back then, we had the old digital answering machines that had digital displays that read the number of messages, and those answering machines would beep to let you know you have voice messages to check.

The message machine was located in our kitchen next to the phone on the wall. My mom went into the kitchen and exclaimed, "What is this? Why are there forty-two messages!" I had gone upstairs to change out of my church clothes and get into my athletic sweats, and my mom screamed out, "Tray, come down here." I came downstairs and asked what was going on. She pressed the button and all forty-two messages were recruiting coordinators from all the top coaches and schools around the country, and we listened to each one, back-to-back-to-back. We all just looked at each other and knew that this was it. My dream of playing Division 1 football was real. My high school recruitment was unprecedented in our family. I was a preseason five-star high school All-American—every player's dream, but with that, I also became a target, and what I thought would be the start of a promising dream season became a nightmare.

THE TRAUMA

What comes along often with this type of notoriety and exposure is the stress of jealousy, racism, scrutiny, and judgment of others. Oftentimes, we want fame and fortune and think it will all be gravy and that everyone will be happy for us. It's naive to assume everything will be roses, but because I was on my way to achieving the prize, and as I was being recognized for my talents, I thought I was prepared for the road of stardom.

The target on my back wasn't just the bullseye; it felt like an entire dartboard. It all started in the summer of 1993 when we began to do our normal off-season football programs. It was time for the seven-on-seven passing league tournaments again.

Our team was always in the A bracket of these tournament games, being that we won three of the last four C.I.F. championships. We were the standard of high school football in the county and were now recognized in the state and country. I always had reporters around or scouts or just fans watching our team that year more than the others because, as one of the best players in the state, other players from other schools would size me up, noticing that I wasn't the player who had the large frame as I was not muscular yet. Rather, I had very scrawny legs, and in pads, I may not have looked so intimidating.

But players would try to intimidate me anyway with yelps like, "I can't wait until we get the pads on! I am going to break you!" and all kinds of trash talk. None of it bothered me at all because my mental game was superb, plus it was just trash talk to me that I never took personally. I never responded to that in kind, but when it came to my actions on the field, they spoke for themselves. After the scrimmage, one of my teammates brought over a player from another team that we had on our schedule for a regular preseason game where the game would be somewhat meaningful, but the game would be played in full pads. As my teammates and I would all rest and refuel somewhere, mostly in the shade under a tree so that we could get out of the summer heat, this player came over to the middle of our huddle. I thought he was a lineman because he was about 5 foot 8 inches and 240 pounds. He came specifically to me and said, "You are Tray Crayton?" I responded in the affirmative, and he said, "I can't wait to light you up, and I am going to do this in front of your fans, school, and recruits. You don't look like one of the best players in the country. You're too small to tackle me—if we meet in the game, I'm running you over." He continued, "If we meet in the hole, I will run you over." I said, "Bet. I will make sure I make that happen."

Normally, I would have just brushed it off and kept it moving. I asked one of my teammates if he knew who this guy was. He told me his name and the team he played for and that he was a running back. As he lingered, I added that I thought he was a lineman, as a dig, and he continued his banter but failed in his attempt to intimidate me. I figured I had to get used to this type of behavior and the negative attention. I was never big on being a fist fighter, but I also did not like anyone in my personal space or challenging my toughness on the field.

At every seven-on-seven where I saw this guy, he would get his verbal jab in and announce that he looked forward to scrimmage day. I probably saw him four or five times that summer. I never said anything else to him that summer while he chirped. As the season crept closer, the anticipation of my senior season grew. I was ready to finalize the season of a very hard-earned legacy that I worked so hard to achieve along with my final year of high school before I set on my dreams to deliver my school another championship. Like my predecessors before, it was important to me to deliver a championship on my own, being it was my team alone. I can compare the pressure and the desire like Kobe winning without Shaq...the best can do it on their own.

I did not boast to my friends about all the preseason hype that was going on. They did not know that I was having interviews with newspapers, recruiting photo shoots, all sorts of media outlets and guest appearances on talk radio stations, among other things. All this was on top of my duties of preparing for the season, practices and all my other obligations, and summer school, as I still had to qualify for the NCAA. I had just turned seventeen years old and was in the spotlight. After traveling under the microscope and after my final year of Hell Week, the fall football camp arrived. We got to put on our pads and practice for the real games against other competition.

The first and only preseason game was here, and I was ready physically and mentally. Since the practices are closed to the public, this is the team's debut, so family, friends, and fans get their first look at the chemistry of the team. The game was at our field, but regardless of being home or away, my family traveled and was always present at both my home and away games. They would walk this journey with me as they knew this season came with a mark on my back.

The scrimmage was going well, and in this type of game, we kept score, but it didn't count toward our win-and-loss column, so every player got to play so that they got a chance to secure or win their position on the team. The returning or new players who started, or players who knew that they would be an intricate part of the team, didn't get to play as much, as a strategy to preserve our starters from being hurt before the games count.

We got to the part of the scrimmage where each team gets something like twenty plays on the goal line. At our school, we had an offense and defense position, and on defense, I played the safety position, which is the QB position. On defense, I called the plays as well. Facing the other team's huddle and formation, I noticed the player from the summer who talked so much trash was in, and I was ready and eyeing. As their QB said hut, the QB tossed the rival player the ball, a hole was created, and it opened up and manifested for just him and I to collide. I ran through the hole like a missile and drilled him. I hit him so hard that he flipped. I screamed, "Whooo!" and I stood over him, saying some not-so-kind words I can't repeat. After my teammates and I celebrated the stop and one of the top moments of the game, I ran off the field, hyping the crowd. My father, who didn't normally bother me in a game, called me over to the fenced area. At this point, I was not sure why he was gesturing to me to come over. In front of everyone in the stands, he grabbed my helmet by the face mask in an aggressive manner and began to drill me about sportsmanship. He reminded me that scouts from Florida, Texas A&M, Oregon, and the like were in attendance, not only watching me play but also watching my character.

I respect my dad so much, and so does everyone else, because they already know his reputation as a minister and a father. I did feel a little embarrassed at the time, and I did consider the consequences of my action, but with respect to my position as the leader of my team, I accepted having to watch how I played, and I had to play a different brand.

One thing I wish I was able to express to my dad was that I endured more than my share of self-control, and I did the right thing during the summer. I didn't talk trash, but I wanted to unleash all the trash talk from this player and others all summer long. I did what I did, and I handled it on the field, and if I still couldn't express it on the field, which was my safe haven due to constantly being in the public eye of judgment, how could I express myself, not push this down, and release my frustrations?

I don't know if that incident gave others the boldness to begin the scrutiny to my face, but from that point on, some of the parents on my high school team and also the teachers from my own team started to talk. Parents started to tell me at pregame meals that they didn't feel I should be getting all the attention I was getting and that this was not just "Tray's team or the Tray show."

One family, in particular, whose son was a teammate of mine since our Pop Warner days, began to come up to me and speak to me with racist remarks. I had to not only fight those who opposed me from the other side but also endure more scrutiny in my own camp.

At first, I didn't want to tell my family. For one, I thought it would end after the first couple of times, and I didn't want to talk back to them, as I believed it would create some friction between myself and one of my teammates. But it got really bad, so I had to address it with my family.

I am a teammate first, always have been, and always will be, and as the captain of our team, I try to act as such. My goal was to always keep the team together as one first. These incidents began to get out of hand when my family was not around at the pregame meals. Multiple moms began to join in with the leader and say smart remarks before the games. I told my mom, and as a result, my mom coordinated with the mother of one of my best friends to make sure I had enough to eat and that she would be the only one to make me a plate and hand it to me so that I can concentrate on getting prepared for the game. So she was the only mom to fix my plate each Friday before I headed to the locker room or the bus, and she did this the entire season.

My family handled the situation in the stands with that one particular family, but the damage was done. My teammate and I played well together but now limited our interaction to the needed communication on the field.

In addition to the racially motivated drama from some of my team's families, some of the teachers and staff members got involved as well and judged me on being an athlete and not a student-athlete. I took my education seriously, but a lot of people had me under a microscope because of the accolades I received outside the classroom. I was not a class clown, nor was I ever late for school or to class, and I was an excellent representative off the field. I was judged solely on my athletic ability. I never had been arrested or in trouble; I had a clean record. I even felt some heat from my head coach.

Our relationship was good, and we had been really close, but as my recruitment and the accolades became more frequent, and with the talks that revolved around me being the star and multiple mentions in the local paper, I felt attacked by the jealousy from him. My parents and my siblings knew this, but the others from the outside didn't know what was going on with our relationship. My teammates never knew that our legendary coach and I had turmoil and that I had to suppress that type of relationship because our relationship became toxic.

I was now overcome with a feeling of being alone in the process of having to battle with my own coach, the families of some specific players, some of my own players, some teachers, school staff members, including the principal at my school. I had to persevere and press on even harder to achieve my goals, no matter the difficult circumstances.

I would get benched for some of the quarters of the game for no apparent reason from our coach, which hurt my ability to perform in front of the scouts. But I couldn't say anything so as to not jeopardize my ability to play on the field so that I could move forward after high school. I was still having a phenomenal season personally, and we were having a good season, but not the seasons of the past. In my senior season, I had lost more games than in my entire career. We had to really battle to still position ourselves for the playoffs. We were about to play one of the biggest games of the season that would determine another league title.

Just before that game, there was a rumor that the opposing team spread about some type of bomb threat to our team bus. Not knowing if this was true or not, we boarded the team bus and got to the game and visitors' field safely. But for me, there was a situation that was real, and there was a threat to my life if I decided to play in this game that would set our postseason goals for both teams in play. Now, this had become real and not a game. The security said to me, "If you play in this game, there could be an active shooter aimed specifically at you." So once we made it to the visitor's field, I was instantly met by some of the field's security guards who were assigned to escort me to the field due to the threat of bodily harm toward me. At that point, I knew this was not a game.

I was definitely naturally concerned for my safety and, yes, a little afraid, but again, I couldn't let my fears get the better of me or rule over my faith not to play and show up. I sat at the other end of the locker room and waited for my parents to get to the game. It was their custom to arrive early, so I asked security to go get them and let them know what the situation was and that I needed to talk to them.

My mom and dad came to the front of the locker room, and I was in full pads, with my head in my hands. Although I said some prayers and knew the promises of protection, my parents could see the nervousness on my face. I looked up just as they turned the corner into the locker room, and since I was away from the team, we were all to ourselves. They both walked with so much confidence in the room, like the Holy Spirit was strutting toward me, but it was my father. The first thing out of his mouth was, "Hey, do you want to play?" I said, "Yeah." So, we prayed, and they said, "God is our refuge and our shield; He will protect you." Who would think to count a situation like this "joy"? When you trust God because you recognize He has been faithful all your life, no matter what man thinks to do to harm you, you get to choose whether it will steal your joy, peace and mental well-being or not. And for me...it was an *or not!*

I walked out with the team and, from a distance, had one security guard accompany me on the side. I was scared, but I knew after our prayer, God was with me. So, I played in the game. None of my teammates or coaches knew that I had to fight through those types of off-the-field battles. Mentally, I was battling and enduring so much pressure to hide what I was going through, and the internal battle to have a great season was weighing on me. I felt like the entire season was my legacy, not any of the years before, but my last year. The pressure and the battle of my mind were not normal to talk about back then. You couldn't express like you may be able to presently because the world did not accept what they would call weak-minded football players. Our persona is "be tough." I had to perform through all these battles, with players' parents, school faculty, and my head coach all opposing me at one time. Our coach was a good coach. I just couldn't wrap my head around why I sensed so much jealousy from him.

Recruiters would call me and let me know that my coach was calling me a showboat and other things that did not align with my character and that I didn't display on the field. The other coaches I played against let those same recruiters know that they thought I played the game with integrity. I never confronted my coach about it because I was already going through a lot with the families and the faculty. I just did my best to stay humble and out of harm's way at school as much as I could.

Nonetheless, I was still getting suspended for things that did not make sense. Still being held out for quarters and disciplined for things I can't explain. In the last game of the season, I sustained a bad injury right before the playoffs. Since I wasn't slated to play in that game, and we were hosting a home playoff game against an inferior opponent that we were confident we were going to win, my coach and I discussed with my family that I could go take one of my five official allotted visits to visit Texas A&M. This school was quickly rising to be the front runner for me to commit to and it was against their rival Texas.

I picked that trip not only because of the timing but also because one of my teammates received a scholarship and he had become a true freshman starter. Due to NCAA rules, the school could only pay for my flight, but my family wanted to go check out the school with me. So we planned it, and my family was set to drive out on a Tuesday in order to get there in time so that we could tour the school and attend the Thursday night game and atmosphere together. I then would fly back to be on time for the game that I was already out for while I still was recovering due to the lingering injury.

The day before my flight, all of a sudden, my coach called me into the office after our weight session and told me it was not fair if I went on the official visit and that if I left and missed practice, I was going to be kicked off the team, giving me an ultimatum. I advised him that my family was already en route to Texas so they could meet me there the next day and that the university and the coaches were expecting me.

I couldn't just call my parents as we didn't have any cell phones or any type of communication like the present. There I was again, having to make a crucial choice, and I felt like it was done on purpose, trying to show that I was a selfish type of player and individual. I had no choice but to go on the trip, as I believed it was necessary for my future. I told my parents when we got to the campus, but we maintained that God would work it out. But when I got back from that recruiting trip, the coach had emptied out my locker and told the team that

I chose my future of being on the team. I was hurt and embarrassed as it appeared to my teammates that I had quit. I had to talk to my teammates and let them know that wasn't the case.

When I got to the bus to travel with the team, only one of the coaches let me ride with them, and I had to observe from the stands instead of participating and trying to contribute support on the field. That was very tough for me, watching from the stands; we were playing the highest seed in the playoffs, and I wanted nothing more to be out there with the team. We won the game, and I was happy, but as the time began to run out, and as the stands began to chant in victory, I began to hear a family of one of my teammates start to chant, "Tray who!" in the stands during the celebration. Being on the field, I never heard it, but hearing it personally like that really crushed my spirits in that moment.

As we were ready to go to the semifinal game, the team had to hold a separate meeting without me, and the coach held a vote to see if they would vote me back on the team. Since I got ahead of the misconceived notion that I had just left for the recruiting trip as a selfish act, my teammates knew my character and understood that was not the case and that the truth was so far from that. I was reinstated to the team. In the semifinal, the coach didn't start me again for the entire first quarter.

We fell behind and were losing ten to zero, and at the beginning of the second quarter of the game is when

I got to make my first play from scrimmage. I scored the first play, and we slowly began our comeback. This game was so important to my life, and I didn't want it to be my last. I played my heart out, and I ended up playing one of the best games of my life. I also made the game-saving interception that sent us back to the championship. I was so emotional. After every game, I always shook the opposing coaches' hands, as that was a custom that my family did to show respect to our advisors or leaders. I did that, win or lose. There it was—we were set to play the team that I got hurt against and who had blown us out three weeks prior.

When you let go and let God, things come around, and the tests before you, God gives you the ability to conquer. So, just as the season started with the summer and God allowed me to have the losses come full circle, I felt this was the final chapter of such a hard-endured season. We were underdogs for the first time in my career for a championship game, a space I had never been in before. We won that game convincingly, and since the game was televised, I garnered a lot of accolades, but I was just happy to have ended the season as a champion. I finished my high school football career as one of the top fifty players in the country, named by the best high school football publicists (Tom Lemming and Max Emfinger), achieved my goal, and became an All-American (*SuperPrep* and *Blue Chip Illustrated* magazines) All-State, All-C.I.F., and All-League teams. I was invited to play in a lot of All-Star high school games that showcased the top senior recruits. I had all the top colleges and top college coaches around the country come to my hometown and personally speak to my family during in-home visits to persuade me to join their football program. After all the ruckus of entertaining recruiting representatives week after week, month after month, and after all the trips to the different university and campus tours, from east to west, I finally sat down with my family and decided to end my recruitment. Three weeks before the deadline for all student-athletes to decide and sign our National Letter of Intent, I made it public that I would be attending the University of Nebraska, one of the best and most traditional, well-known football programs in America.

Now, I was at the very end of my senior year and had begun to get ready for events like prom and all the other senior activities. Right before the prom, as I was nearing my departure for Nebraska, I was still having issues and battling with some of the school faculty. But since I had really focused on football, my mom took care of the faculty drama, and we always had a plan to make sure that I had college prep courses and the right tutors to help me in the classroom. I had taken the appropriate courses to align with the NCAA eligibility rules. Among those rules, your GPA had to be strong and elective classes were no longer enough to get you into college. As athletes, we needed to have similar GPAs to other students who were applying for four-year universities.

There was one last obstacle on the academic side, and that was the ACT or SAT, which you had to pass to receive the scholarship. I really struggled with math, and to pass this test, I needed a tutor. I worked hard and passed the ACT, and it seemed I had a clear path for me to enroll at Nebraska in the fall. Maybe three weeks before I graduated, my mom got a call from the assistant athletic director from Nebraska who called with bad news.

He said that I needed to get a B in geometry to be eligible as a true freshman when I enrolled at Nebraska. If I didn't, I would have to be a Prop 48 player, which meant I could enroll at the school, but for the first year, I wouldn't be on scholarship. Here was another mountain, another obstacle that I had to face to get to my dream of playing in Division 1 football. I currently was passing my class, but I was barely below the grade I needed to be safe with my scholarship. My mom and I went to the geometry teacher and discussed the situation with her so that maybe I would be able to make up an assignment or something that was fair. She stated that she would think about it, and then she waited until the last days before graduation to let us know that I wouldn't be able to take a test or make up any assignment for any type of extra credit even though I was not far away from the grade I needed.

Here I was again put in the same position but now off the field. Scared and not letting anyone see my disappointment and fear, I had to get ready for one of the biggest accomplishments of all our lives, which is graduation day. On the day of graduation, the assistant athletic director from Nebraska called my mom and delivered the news that made us shout for the victory that we know came from God. He went all the way back in my academic records and found a class that I took as a freshman, a college prep math class that would allow me to replace and substitute my geometry grade. He allowed me to use that grade on my transcript, so I was able to keep my scholarship and begin my career and my dream.

CHAPTER 6

The Cracking Walls of the World

The summer of 1994 was awesome! I was just taking it all in about where I was headed. I really did not date too much; I didn't really have a girlfriend, not that I didn't want to; I just was really focused on having that when I got to college. Since I knew I was eventually going to leave, I didn't get serious with anyone, but after I signed and my high school career was over, I got out a bit more. I started dating in the last quarter of high school. She came to our school at the end of our senior year. We came together and talked a lot about staying together through my years in college.

I was scheduled to report to Nebraska's fall camp at the end of July. It was earlier than all the other football teams because we were invited to play in the 1994 NCAA Kickoff Classic in New York City at the NFL stadium of the New York Giants. It is the annual first nationally televised game of the season, and we were ranked number one.

Oceanside celebrates Juneteenth annually at our beach and at our pier. The entire city, it seemed, would come together for parades, concerts, and the arts and to honor the cultural reason of freedom from slavery. I also knew this would be the last time I'd see everyone from the community before I headed off to Nebraska for football camp and to officially move on campus.

My brother Chris and I planned to go to the pier together with a couple of our friends but not stay there too long. I really just wanted to say goodbye to all my family and friends who supported me. And since my whole family planned to go, most of my cousins and other family members were already down there. We went later in the day. We hung out for a little bit and walked around briefly before we ran into my big cousin, Kevin. Kevin, who stood 6 foot 5 inches, was super handsome and was also very connected in our community. He had always stood out and was pretty much the leader of all the cousins.

As we always do when we see family, when we rolled up and approached Kevin, we showed love and did the family hug. The first thing out of Kevin's mouth was, "Hey, how long are you guys going to be around?" and we let him know that we were about to roll out right then to go home. He would always make sure to let us know that if we needed anything or a ride, he would take care of us because he had the entourage to do so. Chris and I really did go straight home after our interaction with him.

We got home about an hour after seeing Kevin, and when we walked into the house, Chris and I were laughing or coming into the house normally until my mom told us to come into the back room.

She looked really distraught, and it was clear she had been crying. We both asked what was going on. She said that Kevin had just been murdered. He was shot and killed during the Juneteenth event that we had just left. In shock and disbelief, Chris fell to the ground, and I said, "Mom, no way, we just saw him; we were with him before we walked in the door; he just told us to be safe."

Kevin was the closest of my cousins to us; we lived with him briefly before we moved into the house that we were in, and we all shared the garage room together. We would go to his house to play video games, and he was always around. He was the rock to all the cousins. Living in the Deep Valley and in Oceanside, we had our share of murders among our peers, but this time, it was hitting home. He was my aunt's—whom I love so dearly—only son.

It was beyond devastating news. It was the first time that our family would be rocked by a murder, and death was such a blow to our family and my heart. It was the first time this type of senseless crime hit our name. It was the first time in my life that I would be a pallbearer and have to deal with that type of internal pain. Three weeks after dealing with Kevin's death, which was still fresh to me, I had to pack up and leave my family at such a difficult time, as it was time for me to leave for Nebraska. I wish I was able to grieve more with my family, but I couldn't. I would have to push my feelings aside and concentrate on moving away from my family, but I just missed him so much that I would cry alone as I tried to concentrate on the start of the new season of my life.

When people say things just begin to rain, but then it pours, that was indeed happening. Now, I was preparing to leave, and it was two days before my flight to Nebraska. As I was packing my bags, I got a call from my girlfriend. Normally, we talked, so I thought it was not a big deal for her to call me. Of course, she called and told me that we needed to talk and to meet her on the corner of our streets because we lived right around the corner from each other. I thought she just had cold feet that I was about to leave and needed to see me and get some assurance that we were making a good decision to stay together. After a long hug, she gave me an envelope and inside was a piece of paper. It was a sonogram, and at that very moment, she broke the news to me that she was indeed pregnant.

The first thing we both decided was not to have an abortion, then after we discussed keeping the baby—there was no doubt at all about not having him no matter what. Since I was about to leave in two days, I had to figure out how I was going to tell my parents while I made the short walk home. I remember knocking on my parents' door to tell them the news.

I came to the side of the bed where my mom and dad were preparing for bed, and I just said it—no warning. I just blurted it out. My mom just had a look on her face like no way, not in disappointment but that I was so close to leaving for school; what other news could we receive, especially still dealing with my cousin's death after we had been through all the other things involving football and school. The first thing she asked was, "Are you going to stay home or go to school?" They were very supportive of whatever my decision would be, but I told her that I decided to still leave and go to school and that we would try our best to do this the right way, although we were going to be young eighteen-year-old parents. I know my mom was relieved that I was not going to find a way to manage fatherhood and continue to pursue my education and my dream of playing pro football, but they both knew what it takes to raise a young child at the age of eighteen and that it is by no means a walk in the park.

So now I had the death of my favorite cousin and the news that I was going to be a father at the age of eighteen. It was tough to leave my family, and I felt the pressure of what people were going to think and say about me, leaving my pregnant girlfriend and going to a different city on my own. The judgment of the public eye and the church loomed over me from that point on, and the perception that came with me being a sinner and the judgment of me being a deadbeat dad because I left made me mentally unhealthy. People did not know how much that truly affected my mental health. I always wanted some kind of acceptance that I was a good person and not a selfish and prideful one, but I just couldn't shake this picture that others had of me.

Nebraska was definitely not a place that I thought I would live, but I always thought I would go anywhere I had to so that I could play ball and fulfill my dream. So, the country sights of Nebraska were going to have to do. My brother Chris was at Oral Roberts University but had a strong desire to play basketball at the D1 level. So, we reached out to the Nebraska men's basketball team to see if there was interest in allowing my brother to walk on to the program in hopes of earning his own scholarship. We both believed it would be great for us to be at the university together; at least we would have each other. He put together some highlight tapes, and they let him walk on the team. I would go first to camp, and then Chris would come when school started, as the men's basketball season started later.

I was still relatively very skinny, which became my calling card and always produced doubt when it came to anyone seeing my build and wondering whether I would play tough football.

Obviously, being recruited to the best program in the country, we had to have some skills despite the press and accolades. Everyone still had to prove themselves all over again, especially among these players who were the best of the best.

I was having a great freshman camp on the field, but I never felt I fit in; I was considered a square to some of the new players who came into the class with me.

Some of the freshmen players would tell the other players who didn't know me that I was a sellout, so I would normally sit by myself at the beginning of fall camp. I was sort of an outcast. One thing I could do well, though, was ball. I practiced hard and I always made plays and had the attention and respect of the older players quickly.

A goal of mine was to play as a true freshman in college. Not only was that a superior feat, but I always felt it would secure my way to getting drafted into the NFL. In college sports, the off-season program was even tougher than high school. It's a big business, so preparation for the season was more rigid because games were longer due to TV breaks, and most universities have regular media timeouts that are built into the game, which stretches the game from two hours to four-hour games. Practices were super intense, and everyone there knew how to practice. Again, it was the best of the best around the country. When it came to practice, you practiced, but when it came to the scrimmages, that was the time that we were able to show our game-time awareness. And it was usually the time when you could stake your claim to try and move up on the depth chart or your playing time. Also, in college, they allowed fans to attend sometimes.

The difference between Nebraska and any other school was, and I believe still is, that the Husker fans are top-notch. Their scrimmages were just like the game day atmosphere. Their stadium, which held 90,000 fans in all red, showed up with 90,000 in the stands for games, practice, scrimmages, whatever. It is a sight to see, and that is why the stadium is nicknamed the Sea of Red. I had never played in front of a crowd like that—it was *big-time* football. It was time for our first scrimmage of the year, and I was ready to have my coming out party to the Husker Nation. It was to the coaches' surprise that I had a tremendous first scrimmage. I thought I was going to be able to get on the field my freshman year, and I wanted that so bad. However, the coaching staff was concerned that my skinny frame would not be able to hold up in the Big Eight Conference (now known as the Big 12), one of the toughest leagues in the country.

I knew I could play, but they wanted me to be in the weight room to get bigger. So here I went again, being judged because of my stature, and I felt my toughness was being questioned. I had other opportunities to have a guaranteed spot to play as a true freshman with the other schools that recruited me, but I wanted the ring. I didn't realize how not being able to play for a whole year would impact me. Playing football is what made me happy. With being away from home, in a new part of the country, and feeling out of place, I needed to play.

To compensate for not playing and having so much on my mind, like still dealing with leaving my pregnant girlfriend, my family that protected me, and being alone in my thoughts, I began to go to college parties with my freshman teammates who were red-shirting like me. There were only two of us out of the class who played as true freshmen, and one ended up being a top-ten pick in his respectable draft. As a matter of fact, this player and I were the only two players that they thought about not red-shirting because we had great fall camps, but his frame was ready for a full college season.

I started to cope by drinking more at parties and going out more on the weekends because there was nothing else to do on campus. It was not the best course of action for someone in my position, but I had no one to talk to to try to keep me encouraged about what to expect if I continued to press through; no one in my family had ever experienced getting this far. I began to party, and things slowly began to spiral downhill for me mentally. Chris and I didn't see each other as much as we thought, as our respective practices had our schedules out of sync.

We ran into each other on this giant university campus, but it was mostly at the training table, which is where all the athletes in all sports ate, but he still was in a different dorm. I was trying to juggle being homesick and not playing football while still trying to figure out how I was going to be a father from so far away.

Like the other freshman players who were in my position, I played on the scout team. We would prepare our teammates in regard to the plays and schemes for that week. I still practiced hard and got much respect from the older players because of the way I played and practiced. We made it through the regular season undefeated, and we were ranked number one and headed to Miami to face the number three-ranked Miami Hurricanes (known as The U) in the FedEx Orange Bowl for the National Championship. This was the experience that I had dreamed of my entire life. I was eighteen and getting ready to play in one of the most historic bowl games in college football.

We won the National Championship in my first year in college, and that was goal number two of the triple ring completion tour. I got through the first season without playing in a single game, and I had not done that my entire life. Although I got the ring that year, I was always the star, and it was the hardest adjustment for me. I would later realize that all high school players have to suffer from being the star to playing as a role player, but until you experience it, it is hard to understand this growing pain process. This had been such a tough year for me mentally, not playing in a game, not playing in front of the 90,000-plus fans that I dreamed of playing in front of.

Another reason why I chose Nebraska is because, at the time, Nebraska was known for having the best facilities and the premier strength and conditioning coaches in all of college football. They were the best, and they were legendary.

Nebraska had the money and all the resources to turn you into a chiseled athlete with speed, power, and rapid acceleration. There was a new strength and conditioning coach that they had hired in the off-season. He came from the Big Ten Wisconsin program, and he had a resume for growing athletes' physical attributes.

They put me on a program that required me to meet with this coach at 5 a.m., eat specific meals, and endure being pushed to my limit. I had to be disciplined and dedicated as this was a specific weight plan individualized just for me. The goal was to gain 30 pounds in four months...this would involve a huge increase in my food and protein intake, but I was up for the challenge.

Nebraska is cold, with nothing to stop the snow. There are no mountains, hills, or anything else to get between you and the elements when it comes down. It just envelops its surroundings.

I had to walk through sleet, snow, and the darkness traveling from my dorm over to the stadium, which was about four or five blocks. And in the Midwest, blocks are not like the city blocks I was used to...it was about a two- or three-mile walk.

Sometimes, it was so cold and windy that I would have to walk backward so that the chill would not freeze my face. I was always determined to do what it took to be the best, so I just did it; I had to.

I was so focused on getting my weight and my body ready for the spring ball camp; that was all I wanted to do, and it would also keep my mind playing during the upcoming season. I also wanted my newborn son to see his father play in front of the sights and sounds of Division 1 and, in the near future, NFL fans. But I was still alone and had spent too much time with my own thoughts. I was so far away from home, and I really missed my family.

The coach who recruited me would check on me from time to time. He would call me into his office and ask me how I was doing, but I never told him the truth. I hid my feelings all the time because that's what I believed I should do as an athlete. I never expressed my feelings of fear or loneliness or exposed my sensitivities. It was just tough to get through. I had to keep reminding myself of my goals and remembering my purpose for being there.

You normally form a great bond with the coach that recruits your area as a high school player because they are the person that you mostly speak to about information and questions as you navigate your way through the recruiting process, so when you get to the school, you have a form of contact with him as well as that coach with your family too. When the coach that recruited me caught me looking really sad, and it could easily be seen at times that I was having a very difficult time adjusting to being alone, he would mention my family or that he spoke to my mom, and he knew that would bring a smile to my face.

One day, as I got up for my routine workout plan for the morning, the coach sent an assistant down to tell me that he wanted to see me in his office.

As I approached the halls of the football offices, the staff seemed different; they all seemed to just have their heads bowed low, not in a disrespectful manner, just solemn. I arrived at the office and entered as I normally would. Seeing my coach, I said, "What's up, Coach? You sent for me?" Coach replied with news I could never be ready to hear or prepared for. He then proceeded to let me know that my grandfather had passed away, and they allowed me to call my parents from the football office. It was just a month or so earlier that he witnessed me win a collegiate National Championship. He was so proud of me.

I was devastated again, but this time, I was not around my family to help grieve at the moment. I cried and cried right there in my coach's office and was consoled by every staff member in the office. This is my grandfather I was named after, my biggest fan. I was his superstar, and he was mine. I never got to go home because the constraints of collegiate athletics restricted the opportunities for leisure travel, especially in the middle of an academic semester.

However, under the bereavement rules of the NCAA, I was allowed to return home under these special circumstances. I now had just buried two of my closest loved ones in less than one year, first my cousin Kevin and now my grandfather, Clarence Crayton Sr., aka "Papa."

It was not the ideal way that I wanted to get home, but I was ready to see my family and my girlfriend, who was very close to having my firstborn son. I had not seen them for about seven months.

What a tough week that was. I was a pallbearer for my grandfather, the second time that I had the honor in the span of a year. Leaving my family again after a short stay would prove to be far more difficult than I had imagined. Being surrounded by so much support and love, going back to the state of isolation awaiting me in Nebraska really took its toll on me and my mind again, and I was not in a good place. But I had to remain mentally tough and go back to do what must be done to accomplish my hopes and dreams.

Tyler, my son, was set to arrive in April, the same month as the spring ball and special spring practices that the university set aside to prepare the new teams for the upcoming year. This is a time when we jockey for positioning on the depth chart. We are under strict evaluation to increase our playing time and even fight for the open positions left by the upperclassmen who graduated or had entered the NFL draft.

I was in a great position to compete for significant playing time. I had worked harder than I ever had to posture myself where I needed to be to impress the coaches. I put in the mental work as well as the physical work. I had gained the weight I needed, and I was faster, stronger, and bigger than ever before.

I went from 150 pounds to a chiseled 190. I gained 40 pounds of muscle and increased my speed, agility, responsiveness, and power. It showed when it was time to demonstrate my growth, and I had moved up on the depth chart to the number two safety position...behind a senior.

Our final two scrimmages were set, and we had one more week left until the final Red and White Scrimmage. I had already had two phenomenal scrimmage evaluations. I was in the scrimmages up against the starters. On one particular play, I tackled the preseason Heisman Trophy running back, who was powerful and fast.

I tackled him, but I had to get up fast and get back into position because we were going through our two-minute drill, which is the hurry-up offense, so I had to look over to the coach as my position had to call the coverage for the secondary. I was screaming out the coverage with my voice and the hand signal. It was a simple Cover 0, which means we were man-to-man across the field.

I looked to my right and put up two fists from one side of the field to the other. The corner on my right-hand gets the signal, but the corner on my left continues to yell, "What's the call?" I was screaming, "Cover 0," with my left hand in a fist. He got even more animated, screaming out to me, "Stop playing, what's the call?" So, I looked at him directly, looked at my fist, and said, "Cover 0!" I didn't realize that my middle finger was sticking up at him, and I couldn't feel it sticking up at him. I looked as if I was flipping him off, which explained why he was getting so upset. As soon as I saw my hand, I ran toward the sideline, straight to the trainers. After a quick evaluation of my finger, they diagnosed me with a rupture of the flexor tendon.

I had no idea what that was. I later learned it is the tendon that gives our fingers the ability to bend. That's how powerful the force was from when I grabbed the jersey of the running back to bring him down; it ripped my hand. I had to have immediate surgery to repair my finger.

I was having such a great spring, and there was something else in that year that went wrong, another setback. I never ever had surgery or any problems with my body. I was not used to being injured or having to deal with not being on the field for a significant amount of time. They say the higher you go, the more you'll have to deal with injuries. But it's hard to prepare for. All athletes battle through bruises, sprained ankles, and jammed fingers.

But when it comes to surgery and recovery, it is different. I practiced the last week with my hand wrapped up in a protective club, and I played the final scrimmage with one hand.

To be honest, I really didn't want to practice or play because it was so uncomfortable to play with one hand, but in the world of football and sports, we are expected to play through all types of injuries. It's been said, "If you can walk, then you can play." That is the tough mentality you grow into, and you do it no matter what. So that's what I did, but because I was out the prior year, I wanted to do whatever I could do to show my toughness, and I worked so hard that I didn't want to sit out another year.

Tyler was set to be born a week after I tore my left hand, and I wanted so much to be there for the birth of my firstborn. I was able to come back for a week in order to try and fit it inside his due date, but I had to get back because I had to have the surgery within a certain time period, or it would make matters worse for me to be able to use that finger again.

My girlfriend didn't begin labor until my last two days at home, and Tyler was born the night before I had to leave to go back to Nebraska. It was simply incredible and one of the best days of my life. I was just turning nineteen years old, and I was a brand-new father. Somehow, all the bruises, surgeries, and challenges I was facing paled in comparison to the miracle of becoming a dad.

I knew that I only had a couple of hours with him, so I stayed up all night holding him, talking to him, and expressing my devotion to always being there and never leaving him. I felt really uneasy because physically, I had to leave him, but it was only because I also wanted the best opportunity for us to be well taken care of through the financial opportunity the NFL would bring.

I had to leave so quickly, and I know it was hard on me, but it also would be hard on my girlfriend. I had to say my goodbyes and get back to Nebraska. My brother

Chris picked me up from the airport and transported me straight to surgery. I remember telling him that I was nervous because I didn't like the doctors putting me to sleep. Chris said he would be there waiting for me and be there the entire time. The surgery went well, but there was something interesting that happened. I woke up from the anesthesia during the procedure.

I did not feel anything, but I was conscious. The doctor and the team quickly let me know I was still in surgery, and I looked to my left, but there was a small barrier between my shoulder and hand that cut off the sight to my left hand. The doctor said to me, "Hey, this is very unusual for someone to wake up from the anesthesia, so would you like to see your hand while it's open?" I thought, *Heck yeah!* This is something that I would never see or experience again.

He lifted the veil so that I could see my hand, and OMG! I saw my hand completely open with my exposed skin pinned to a board in the manner of a stretched, dead snakeskin. I could see my flesh and the skeletal makeup of my finger. From that point on, there was no need for any more anesthesia because I passed right back out after that, and I am sure that the doctors, whoever and wherever they are to this day, get a kick out of that.

After some time after the recovery and the physical therapy, I needed time to get my finger back to working and bendable functionality. I lost a lot of rotation in that finger and my hand; it was a big change for me to have to deal with a major injury. I had my arm in a sling for a very long time. I also received my National Championship ring with the sling on my arm. My picture where I received my ring at the ring ceremony is a symbol forever of that event.

Having that injury set me back. I couldn't carry my books or lift the weight that I had improved on so much during the off-season. So much of the off-season work I had done to build all that muscle and strength began to dwindle. I put a lot of pressure on myself mentally, carrying around the knowledge of losing my cousin, not playing, losing my grandfather, leaving my son, and then an unforeseen injury, all within this first year at Nebraska.

I needed help, but I didn't know where to turn to get some peace through what I was dealing with, which was a heavy load again, especially for someone my age.

The pressure went from a rock to a hill, and now it felt like a mountain. It was all becoming a lot of pressure, but all I knew to do was push it down, battle and fight through the feelings.

In D1 football, we normally had to stay on campus the entire year. It was critical that every opportunity was taken to be among the members of the team, build rapport by working out together, and even take some of the same summer classes, so going home was really not an option.

The campus became a ghost town as all the other students prepared to go home for the summer. I had put on a good face, but being so far from home got the better of me, and I began to cave under the weight. I started to act out because I didn't have an outlet. I decided that I just didn't want to be in Nebraska anymore. I knew it wasn't the best decision to leave because it was so close to the season, and I was still in a position to play a lot, and I was second-string as a redshirt freshman, but I just didn't have the knowledge and guidance to make the right decision. I was only nineteen, and I wish I had someone who was in my position to tell me that it would be okay and to stick it out. My family didn't know what I was going through, and neither did I. I found it hard to find the words to explain what I felt.

We were supposed to repeat as champions as well as bring our entire core team back that won the prior year. Our legendary coach at the time called me into his office, and he inquired about my state of mind because he could see that I was drifting.

Being in this atmosphere, you are considered an adult, and you have to make adult decisions. That's why it is good to have support and listen to mentors or others who may have felt the way you do.

I didn't have that because I was the first in my family to achieve and go this far. I told him I just wanted to leave, and I didn't want to be there anymore. He told me to think it over for one night, and if I wanted to leave the next day, he would let me go. I called my parents, of course, and my father, who is very traditional and loving, told us that when we turned eighteen years old, we were adults and to make our own decisions. I really didn't want to do anything but come home, so I didn't really get the talk. I felt like I needed to just stick it out.

It is not his fault at all; I just wished at that time that he would have given me a little more guidance concerning how my decision could impact my future. What I had to come to terms with was that he had already sown the word in my heart. I could hear 1 Corinthians 13:11 (KJV) in his voice, saying, "When I was a child, I spoke as a child, I understood as a child, I thought as a child: but when I became a man, I put away childish things."

I had gone through all the summer workouts and decided to transfer right before the season. So, I came home and left the Nebraska program. I would later realize that I'd wish I had stuck this out, but we make our own choices. God can't make the choices for us.

First, the transfer rules at the time were that you had to sit out a year, so I would lose another year of eligibility. I called all the schools that had recruited me heavily before, but because of the timing of my transfer, no one had open scholarships; they were all filled by the current recruiting class. They wanted me, but I would have to pay for a semester of school before they could put me on a scholarship after the season opened up, and I didn't have the resources to do that, so I would have to find a school with a scholarship.

So, the schools that I wanted to come home to, the Pac-10, were full. Only one school was open with a scholarship, and that was Washington State. I took it because I couldn't afford not to. I struggled there as well, even worse than in Nebraska. I was on an even smaller college campus and while it was not the same program as Nebraska, I did see the potential in their roster.

Not all of my bruising took place on the football field as matters grew worse with my drinking, and I even began to smoke marijuana to deal with my anxieties, stress, and lonesomeness. I rarely went to class and was just completely lost.

I actually flunked out of school there and became ineligible for the first time in my life. All of the doors of opportunity to fulfill my dream of the NFL seemed to not just close but had been slammed in my face.

I decided to come back home and try to regain my confidence and get my life back. I enrolled at a junior college, and I picked one where I could play after not playing in a real game for two years.

I remained in the grace, safety, comfort, and support of my home. Moreover, I was in the peace and blessedness of being able to finally be close to my son.

I had just experienced two of the toughest years of my life where everything I had planned and thought was under control was now tattered, scattered, and shattered, and I was ready to jump off the hamster wheel and stop wasting and losing what I felt was precious time.

Coming home was the best thing for me at the time. Seeing my son every day really helped me put my life back into perspective. My entire life has been faith, family, sports, and love. I was able to gain that back during my years back on the field and being back in my community. I got myself back together at this point.

I got to get back to my love of playing on the field and being a leader, and I had a great season and became a JC All-American. I had some offers to return back to some big-time colleges. I wanted to stay home and attend San Diego State. They elected not to make me an offer, a decision I think was based on me being the journeyman and because, as a high school star, they recruited me hard, but I never really showed interest, so I may have burned that bridge.

I had set up visits to attend programs that were on the national stage, and I desperately wanted to get back to that brand of football.

Nebraska had already won two more National Championships during that time, and that name was always linked to me because I was a part of one and a half of those years.

One of my teammates was going on a recruiting trip to a small school, and it was still a good program but not a tier one.

I remember specifically saying, "No, I'm not going!" I even told the school I was not interested, but they still wanted me to come, which is a tactic some schools use to get a big-time recruit on campus so they can just get them to see the surroundings with their own eyes and persuade them to commit.

This was nothing new to me, as I had been through this process just under three years ago. My teammate was already hyped to go, and I kind of knew he was going to commit to the school. I went very nonchalantly, and they knew I was not interested. They brought out the red carpet, but I was still wanting to get to a nationally televised program, though I knew I didn't have much time left.

One of the other recruits from a different city, whom we met up with before we left to go out, asked if I was thinking of committing there. I told him that I wasn't.

He asked me about where else I had considered or had visited. I gave him the list of possibilities and then turned the tables and asked him where he wanted to go. He replied that he was going to Pitt the following weekend. My reaction was that Pitt sucked, I knew of them, but they hadn't won for about years, and I watched them get blown out on TV seventy-two to zero, so I wasn't that interested. He said, "Yeah, but they get on TV for nine out of the eleven games they play, and they also play Miami, Notre Dame, and Penn State." An added big plus was that they played an annual rivalry game on Thanksgiving Day.

So, he pulled out the schedule, and I was immediately interested. He told me he would put me in contact with the recruiting coordinator.

By the time I made it home, the recruiter called me. He was the same coach who recruited me from another school. Not only that, but I also found out that the assistant athletic director, who was the most influential person in my recruitment to Nebraska, had just taken the Pitt Athletic Director job.

He was someone I knew I could trust. He found out I was interested, and they offered me a scholarship right away. All I needed to do was take a trip to the city, and I did so the following week. Pitt was everything I dreamed of. It was far, but it was a city full of life, and I just fell in love with it. It had a downtown, and the campus was in the city, so I wouldn't be surrounded by just hills and fields. There was more than one movie theater. The things that the other campuses lacked, Pittsburgh had—food, entertainment, things outside of football that I wanted. Plus, it was home to the city of the Black and Yellow, Pirates, Penguins, and the Steelers, and the fan bases there are beyond passionate about their teams in the Steel City.

I was also going to be able to bring my son along with me at some time, too, so that he could live and be a part of my life as I went to school. When I first got on campus, it was different. First, this was definitely not my first rodeo, and I was three years older. Instead of being an eighteen-year-old wet-behind-the-ears student-athlete, I was now twenty-one years old. I wasn't coming in as a high school graduate. I was a bit seasoned, coming in and being enrolled with an A.A. degree, fitting in more with the upper-class players.

The big draw in my decision to Pitt also was the tradition that I did not know they had. The ultimate goal was to get Pitt back to their glory days of football, the nine National Championships, all the D1 All-Americans and Hall of Fame NFL players they have had. Pop Warner actually went to Pitt, so I loved the chance to be a part of a class that had the chance to rebuild something, and building the new foundation into Pitt's new era intrigued me a lot.

Pitt did not disappoint me. It was one of the best decisions I have ever made, and I wish I had the wisdom I did after traveling to the other schools, coming out of my first recruitment. Pitt was everything I dreamed it would be, and I flourished in my first full season. I got to play the likes of Penn State on ABC, Notre Dame on CBS, and again, "The U" on Thursday Night ESPN. Although I was further away from my family, Pitt felt like a family, and my own family was able to watch every game from California. I loved all my teammates, but I specifically met two of my best friends to this day: Jackie Womack from my mom's home state of Mississippi and Terry Murphy from California. We became college roommates after our brief stint in the dorms. We dubbed ourselves 80-7-81, our jersey numbers. This would become a bond that still links us to this day.

We had a first-year coach who came from Ohio State, and the year 1997 was a special season for us. We ended up having a winning record, beat our hated West Virginia rivals in the Backyard Brawl, and sent our program to its first Bowl game in twenty-one years. It was just that special. So, I was back again, back to my love, back to feeling good about getting back on course, and the dream had come alive again.

My senior season at Pitt was filled with the same type of hype that I had from my career in high school. I was in all the major publications, the NFL draft buzz was quickly approaching, I was hanging out at clubs with some Pittsburgh Steeler players and attending functions representing the university, and I was one of the top defenders in the Big East.

I was one season away from getting drafted in the NFL and was highlighted in publications such as *Sports Illustrated*, *The Sporting News*, and other widely published sports and media magazines. Meanwhile, I was receiving letters from sports agents from around the world.

We had a promising season ahead of us because we had put Pitt back on the map. I was proud to be a fixture in what we wanted to accomplish.

I also had a tremendous off-season. I had one of the best strength coaches to ever set foot in football. I have not mentioned many names, but Charles "Buddy" Morris, who will no doubt get me for saying his full name, pushed me back to a high level and beyond when it came to toughness. He called me Clarence, and I called him Charles. I was the only one who was allowed to call him that and vice versa. We just had that kind of relationship.

This man's workouts were legendary. He had only a couple of people on his wall, like Dan Marino and Hugh Green and some other very, very talented people. And it wasn't just because they were famous; rather, it was due to the respect Buddy had for their work ethic.

One day, I noticed my picture on his wall, and he let me know that I had earned it. For me, that was the greatest sign of respect that I am still proud of to this day. And to this day, he is still a figure within his industry and he is still applying his gift in the NFL.

He has been around the best of the best, and to consider me as one of the hardest-working athletes that he has ever met means so much to me.

Right before the season, I was traveling around representing the university at functions doing my guest speaking before we started our season opening camp. Terry, who we call Mizzy, grew up with one of the stars of the New York Jets. We got invited to take a quick train to New York to be guests at the Jets' preseason camp before we started our season in the fall. It was my first time just being in the state of New York, and as this player's guests, we were able to be guests on the field.

Bill Parcells was the head coach, and at the time, Bill Belichick (who now is probably the greatest coach of all time and a six-time Super Bowl champion coach) was his defensive coordinator. Coach Belichick knew who I was. It was like coaches were sizing me up. I did not know at the time that Bill Belichick would become who he is today, but we spent some extensive time together as I got to spend time with the DBs as they practiced. It was amazing to see live in action all the hard work these players put in on this level, and I had the feeling that this could be me someday if I was going to get drafted. It was a firsthand, up close and personal look at life in the NFL. Everything looked great heading into the season.

I started putting more pressure on myself. All I knew was that my plans only included me making it to the NFL. I did not really plan to fall back on anything other than football, although I thought of it. My entire life, I believed I would make it to the NFL, and as I trained and developed and became one of the best players on the field, offensively and defensively, that reality was closer than ever before.

I started to feel some tension to perform like I never had before. Some of the pressure and weight came from knowing some serious decisions would need to be made regarding picking the right agent representation, how I would handle life in the NFL making millions of dollars, and how the like would affect my life and those of my son and my family.

I really got ahead of myself. I began to isolate myself again. I did nothing but put weight on life and about nothing else that didn't involve sports.

The season arrived, and after fall camp, we were set to start the season with a lot of great expectations. We were playing one of the biggest games of the season, our home game against our cross-state rival, Penn State and its legendary Coach Joe Paterno, during prime-time national television on CBS.

My entire family had flown in for this game, and I knew that I needed to have a great game. I usually was so even-keeled that I would have fun before the game. But this time, for this game, I just put so much pressure on myself. To prepare for seeing my family, I had this unusual game face on when they came to the hotel. It just wasn't the real me.

The game was sold out, and the buzz was tremendous. I had made so many plays in the game, but one play we had practiced was the back shoulder pass. It was not widely used and was just being introduced in football. The back shoulder pass is a staple now, and normally, the wide receiver just runs straight down the field, and the QB tries to throw it over his head so that the receiver catches it over his shoulder. It is a very accurate throw, and as a former QB, I threw many of those in my life. But the new way was to throw it at the back of the defender so that it made him turn around to try and stop the pass. We practiced this somewhat, but when you are in practice, the game speed is vastly different than in reality. Of course, you always try to emulate game plans, but playing in the game atmosphere is different.

We were tied in the third quarter, and I was having a great game against their number-one wide receiver, but on this play, as we were running down the field at full speed, I was in the perfect position to either knock the ball down or to make an interception. I was looking into the receiver's eyes, as we were taught to do, and I could tell the ball had been thrown in our direction. I turned around so that I could intercept the ball, and in a split moment, I turned toward him because he began to slow down like it was coming to our backs as we had practiced. However, then the receiver stopped, like he misjudged the ball. I turned and didn't see the ball in the air because it was poorly thrown. When I turned again to locate my opponent, he reached his hand out and made a one-hand catch at his knees. I didn't even see the ball because of the poor throw; he scored a touchdown on that play. It was the first touchdown that I had given up since I was a sophomore in my first high school varsity game over six years ago. I was so hurt that I gave up a touchdown. That play would ultimately determine the final score.

I felt devastated because that was it. I felt that was my play, and I failed. It was just one play, but I felt like I lost the game for my team. I put all that pressure on myself. That legendary coach for Penn State made his way over to me at the end of the game and told me I was a tremendous player. In the interview after that game, I think he stated it was a lucky catch against a great defender, but that didn't eliminate the defeat I felt. I cried in the locker room. When we got to the press conference, they asked me about the amazing catch-and-play. I just made a joke about it and laughed it off, but it hurt. It hurt me deeply.

The public doesn't see what we have to go through when we hide what we really feel at that moment and when we don't have the time to process the disappointment.

That game stayed on my mind for the entire season. I never really let go of that play all season. I could not let it go for years. I let that one play push me into even more disappointing thoughts, and the fear crept in again. I began to believe that I wasn't going to have some of the opportunities that I was hoping for, including my future in the NFL, and I quickly went back to doubting myself, a place I was never used to.

Others close to me did not know that I was dealing with this. How could they when I didn't really know what I was dealing with? Talking to others about our mental attitude during those years still was not really an option, and we could not be as open about the subject. So again, I tried to push through.

NFL scouts have access to be visible at practice, and you know that they are there to watch and critique you. When we had individual drills, the NFL scouts would be right there watching your footwork, practice, attitude, and such. I had no problems there, as I always worked hard and practiced hard, but I could not read their minds or their notes, so it was a nerve-wracking situation for me. Again, the pressure, the fear.

We did not have the year that we expected, and we finished the season two to eight. With successful seasons come many successful accolades. It's just the way of sports. When you win, the team also gets individual awards. So, all the preseason hype I received didn't necessarily put me out, but it didn't help that our season was not good. Again, the pressure began to mount in my head. I told myself, "This is it. You have to make it."

I signed with my agent and began my preparation for the draft. I believed that I was slated at best to go on the second day of the draft, between the fourth and the seventh rounds. I was so happy that I didn't care if I was the last pick. I just wanted to hear my name called.

I didn't have anyone who was guiding me through this as my family and I were in rare territory again and hadn't been in this position before. I just went with what I knew, which was not much. I was told that I could possibly go to my hometown Chargers. I had the privilege of completing a private workout for them before the draft, and they told my agent there might be an opening around the third round. I was hyped to hear that. I met with the staff and got a one-on-one workout that I destroyed, showing my speed, agility, hip quickness, and all the things that I prepared for.

So many emotions ran through my whole being leading up to the draft. Were my dreams about to come true? Was everything that I had envisioned as a child right here at the forefront of reality?

My agent had some very famous athletes on as his clientele, and some were the best NBA players at the time. So, I was beginning to see the type of lifestyle I was going to have as I was sitting on the courtside at games. I had access to the locker rooms and was able to walk up to and speak to high-profile athletes, normally inaccessible, without going through their bodyguards or security.

I had thought of all the things I was going to do. I would help my family and buy them whatever they needed: homes, cars, the list was unlimited. The most important gift I wanted to give was to purchase my father a church, a building that would exemplify the vision that God gave him so many years ago.

Before my senior year of college, I wrote my parents a check symbolizing my faith and commitment to always giving back and tithing. I also have always wanted to pay my parents back for their sacrifice in taking me to practice and coming and supporting me at my games. I wrote them a check for one million dollars and told them, "Hold this; I will make this good one day."

The draft was finally here, and we had prepared a draft party at my parents' house. The night before the draft, my brothers and I planned to chill at their apartment and just relax, talk, and enjoy the process. After my brothers and I shared some close, intimate stories and just took in the moment, I made a pallet on the floor for old times' sake.

I went to sleep in peace, but in the middle of the night, or perhaps very early in the morning, I had the worst dream or the most unusual nightmare. It was very real, and I felt like I was out of body in the spirit realm. I was at the draft, and all the lights and glamour of the NFL were right before me. As soon as they were going to call my name, the entire dream went black, and I woke up in fear with a loud "Noooo!"

I thought I had said it out loud, but no one came running into my room. I remember even rebuking the dream and saying, "Please, Lord, that wasn't what I thought it would be like!" Was it the enemy, the liar playing tricks on my faith? I didn't tell anyone about the dream, although I had a sick feeling in my stomach.

We all gathered at my parents' and waited for the phone to ring. Cell phones were new back then, so the house phone number was given to the teams and my agent. Every time someone called, it was nerve-wracking. My mom wanted the phones clear, so the conversations when anyone called were barely a few seconds in length.

The entire first day went by, and that was the first three rounds. I was nervous about it, but I had thought the first three rounds might have been a stretch. I thought for sure the next day, I would hear my name called. On the second day of the draft, we had church, and we had a birthday party for my niece that had already been planned. I could have gone to help her celebrate, and I should have attended to take my mind off the draft, but I decided to stay home and wait for the call.

I grew more anxious and worried as the time passed. Name after name was being called for the position I played. These were names of different players I knew and had played against. Their dreams were being fulfilled, and all I wanted was to say that I had been drafted by an NFL team.

When the last name was called, and I didn't hear my name, it devastated me to my core. I was in shock, unable to move from in front of the television, although I still had some hope that I would get a call from a team to come to camp. The thought of having my name called made me shed tears. I was frozen in my emotions because I would never get that moment or opportunity again. You have one chance, one shot at the hope of becoming an NFL draft pick. It wounded my ego and bruised my spirit.

I went upstairs to my room and lay there in silence. When my family came home, they knew I was disappointed, and they didn't even have to say anything. In fact, they didn't say a word, they just left me in my room to myself. My mother came in sometime later to console me, so at this time, I shared my dream with my mom, and I asked her why I had that dream. I sat up, and my mom looked at me and told me that she had the same dream that night.

We both cried—I, as a hurt son; she, as a consoling, compassionate mother, looking at her son, knowing there was nothing she could do to ease the pain. We just shared our emotions in silence.

I didn't even get a call to be on someone's roster. At that point, all I wanted to do was be invited to camp. I would settle for being able to put on a helmet even if I didn't make the team. I just wanted to experience, if only for a few seconds, what the locker room in the NFL felt like.

Again, nothing. I tried to pray and wondered, "Why me, God?" Why? I was this heralded athlete all my life... the Pop Warner star, a five-star All-American, MVP, Player of the Year, college award teams, a state and national champion.

Why now? Why couldn't I hold the mantle of being drafted or bearing the most important title of them all... a professional athlete?

I felt so betrayed by God. This was an internal scar that cut deep.

I didn't know what to do next. So, I did what I knew and was trained to do...get up, pick up the pieces, work hard, and plan to find another way to fulfill the dream. Take the long route if I had to. It would be hard to do, but not impossible. There were other leagues out there, like the semi-pro teams. Maybe I could get a look. It was not over! I could still make it because I believed in myself and my abilities just that much.

After a short time, I shifted my mental gears and decided to work even harder. I trained. I stretched. I ate healthier. My body was stronger, faster, and even better than before. I even changed agents. This new agent was local in the San Diego area, and he agreed to help me as he, too, was up and coming.

Finally, I got a shot at some tryouts. These tryouts were not your typical tryouts like back in my high school days. You had to either pay or get invited. These tryouts had about two hundred players at a time, who were all trying to get invited to camp to try for a roster of twenty-two with only two spots available on the team.

You had very little time to show your abilities. You may have gotten five reps to show your skill. We had to complete the normal abilities tests that included the 40-yard dash to gauge speed and agility. If you didn't do well there, they would pull us together and call our names from the pool. If your name was not called, you didn't make it, and we were grown athletes, so you just had to get your bags and leave. This theme continued throughout the entire workout as you went from one skill to the other until it dwindled down to the final players that they were interested in. Then, finally, they met with the coaching staff, and it was a couple of days later before you knew whether you made the cut and were invited to attend camp.

I went through this process a couple of times, working out for the CFL and other semi-pro camps, getting to the end of each tryout and waiting for a call with good news, only to hear the opposite: that I was not invited to the camp.

I was still determined to work harder than ever. Giving up was not an option. It was not in my DNA! After a full year, I went to another camp. It was my best camp. I went through the gauntlet of skills and evaluations again like before, but this time, it all paid off. I got the call to be a part of a first-year team. It was a new, up-and-coming pro league that was sponsored by the TNT network. The team was based in LA, so I could stay home, travel up the 5 North Freeway, and still be home with my son Tyler.

I was the only incoming rookie who had survived all the held tryouts and still was not drafted by the team.

But I finally got another shot.

I wasn't on the team yet, as I still had to survive training camp. It was a paid league, but I didn't get paid as much as the other ex-NFL players on the team.

I had to work my way onto the roster. Each day, there were cuts that brought out a staff member who would come in the morning and knock on your door. He is known in the football world as "the Reaper."

When you had a roommate, and he arrived at the door, it was not immediately known which of you the Reaper was coming for. Once you were identified, the next thing you heard was, "The coach wants to see you. And bring your playbook."

That's all that is said. When this happens, you say your goodbyes to your roommate, who you most likely won't see again. You wish them the best, and you are sent home. That is the way. Each day, this happened for about two or three weeks. Sometimes, it was due to skill set, and other times, it was a numbers game, or it was politics. Then, there's the rare occasion that it mattered who you knew, which could be your saving grace.

I went through this day after day, but I continued to show the skills necessary, so they wanted to keep me. It was a tremendous amount of pressure, but I had the grit to endure.

It feels great to say I made the team! I had made it on a professional team's roster. It may not be what I envisioned, but I continued on with the dream to make it, whatever that took. Our games were held at the LA Coliseum, a place where my brother Garrett, who is a huge USC fan, was excited to see me play.

My entire family had not watched me play for some time, and we always made it a huge road trip event to watch one another play. I was hyped and ready and could not wait to finally play again. I wasn't starting, but I did expect to play. It was encouraging that all my teammates acknowledged my skills and gave me respect as a player both on and off the field.

During this particular game, everyone was getting a chance to play in the game, except me. I was on the sideline, itching and waiting to get called in, even if it was for just one play, especially because my family was in the stands.

For some reason, the head coach did not want to put me in, not even on special teams. I heard my coach tell him to put Crayton in, but he refused. My position coach just shrugged his shoulders, expressing that he, too, was confused about the decision. I just wanted one play, but he was not going to allow it.

We were in the final five minutes of the game. I was told by one of the gunners, the position that punts and runs down to cover and tackle the punt returner, "You have to fight two people and run at full speed down the field."

Before the play started, I ran on the field, and the coach couldn't stop me because, at the last minute, I darted on and got in position. I lined up, using my speed to split the two defenders, and took off.

While the player was looking up to catch the ball, he didn't anticipate me being down the field so fast. Right when he caught the ball, I timed it perfectly and made the biggest hit of the game. The crowd went crazy, and I just pointed at my family, who was going nuts. I pointed at them as if to tell them, "This was for you!"

As I ran off, the head coach came up to me and said he saw my great play. That would be my last play with them, as the next day, the Reaper came into the locker room, even during the season, and let me know I was cut. I wasn't one of the players he drafted. I was the only player on the team not drafted. He did not have any affiliation with me. I had just played so well during camp that he couldn't cut me. So, I was back to the beginning again.

Months later, one of my best friends from my time at Washington State called me and told me that he had heard that I was still trying to get myself into the NFL. He had been to some NFL camps and on some practice squad teams, which are the scout teams for the pros. They only practice but are not on the 53-man traveling roster. He told me about a league called the Arena Football League. He was one of the main stars there, so he said he could get me a tryout.

I took him up on the offer. It was based in LA and was bought by the NFL. It was like a minor league to pick up talent. This league was unique because it was all passing, which could showcase my skills for scouts. I was invited to a three-day tryout. Here I was again, having to show out ahead of other contenders what I could do. My body was ready. My mind was poised for the challenge. I practiced the entire three days and made the team.

They held tryouts every week, so it gave me a glimpse of what professional football is like. If you're not on your game, someone can come along and take your spot, and that is exactly what I tried to do and achieved. I was officially on the roster and in a position to play a year after the other team had cut me.

I was more mentally mature and understood what was at stake. This time, I got to play in the Staples Center, home of the LA Lakers. The AFL was an indoor league that played in famous basketball arenas that were transformed into 50-yard football fields. This game was fast and exciting.

The scores in those games were in the eighties. It was very difficult to stop offenses as the game was geared toward the exciting brand of football, basically scoring as many touchdowns as possible for the fans. The fans were also right there next to you where they could touch you, or you could talk to them on the sides of the field. The only thing that separated us was a board that guys flipped over or collided with when they ran into it. That was the out-of-bounds marker on the wall.

I made it on that roster in the middle of the season. We were playing the defending champions, and in the third to last game, I got to start.

I was having a terrific game, but in the middle of the third quarter, as I was back peddling, I heard my foot pop. I went straight down like I was shot with a high-powered bullet. I got evaluated, and I popped my foot out of place. Yes, you guessed it, another setback.

I had to stay in LA and rehab my foot, and that took about six or eight months. It is part of the process of football. There are pains, injuries, scars, and bruises. Pain comes with the game, and while you may hope it never happens, when it does, you have to endure and overcome.

By the end of my rehab, camp was back in session again and the position coach who was with us the year before had left for a new opportunity with another team in our league. They invited me back to camp, and I signed my first contract that came with better pay...and it was good money.

It was also my first full year in the league, so I was still considered a rookie when it came to contract negotiations. I had a great camp and was set to play a big role on the team. However, two weeks into the preseason, I was informed that I would be leaving the LA team and joining my ex-coach in Oklahoma City.

In this business, you have to be ready for the unexpected. There is sometimes very little time to get things situated, as you could be leaving as early as the next day to get to your new team, city, and life. You have to be willing to change your surroundings abruptly.

I was then with the Oklahoma City Wranglers. In football or any sport, you must learn to adapt quickly to change, new teammates, coaches, etc. You will meet new people, and instantly, some are ready to be for you, and others are not. Nonetheless, you have to remember your why! Remind yourself that because you are playing for yourself, your family, and your livelihood, you must not take anything personally when it comes to others doing what they need to do to win a starting position or the playing time to continue to get paid.

Being traded is not easy, but it happens in sports. People view trades as players just leaving one team for another, but I had to leave my son and get acquainted in another city before I brought him there again.

So, my family helped out until I could send for him to join me. Being a father full-time was difficult. When I had to go on the road for games, there was a lot to juggle, like daycare, preschool, and babysitting, to name a few.

I had a great year, and the scouts were starting to hear about me again, and I was hearing from some NFL teams. After a great rookie season, I felt like things were coming back into place.

Although I had this football career, it wasn't enough income for me, so in the off-season, I had to work odd jobs so that I could make sure Tyler and I were good. I still had to train as well to stay in shape for the seasons ahead. As we embarked upon year two with the team, word spread that our team was among those moving and splitting from the AFL conference realignment.

Our team got sold and now all the teams were able to draft players from those that got dismantled. Here, I was facing another draft. The memories of the NFL and whether I would get my name called came back. I was working at my job the day of the draft, and I received a call letting me know that I had been drafted in the third round by the New York Club. I felt that was surreal in a way because when I was at Pitt, I had gone to New York and thought I would go in the third round to my hometown team. It felt like things had almost come full circle.

Now that I was older, my opportunities for getting picked were drying up, and I knew I had maybe a year or two to get selected. I went to the New York camp and survived for a short time until I was cut again.

Los Angeles heard that I was available, so they invited me back to the team. I had a lot of things on my mind, but the priority was my son Tyler. I was packing up so much that he was not able to get stable in school or develop a sense of community, and I was gone from him far too often.

I told myself that I didn't want to move from California again, and if I could stay with the LA team until I got a shot, then that's what I had to do. Or I needed to come to terms with the fact that my dream and shot had to end soon. I played my last professional football game that year. I had to retire from football and hang up my cleats. I had to make the decision that was best for me and my son. It was not easy, and I had nothing planned, no backup plan of what to do next.

About five or six years had passed at this point and Tyler was beginning to embark on school, and I knew that I wanted him to feel support from me. I wasn't giving up my dream; I just had other responsibilities that took center stage and warranted my undivided attention.

I had to get a job, but I didn't know where to start. As a student-athlete on a full-ride scholarship, it was a violation to receive anything from anyone. There could be no financial assistance, not even one dollar from anyone outside your family, otherwise the entire university would be sanctioned. We were never able to set ourselves up for the reality of the workforce or have any experience like other students who could be involved in internships and part-time work while in school or during the summer.

These were strict NCAA violations, and committing them was largely to blame for why many athletes come out of school unprepared for what's next. Well, at least those whose only goal was to achieve becoming or being labeled an athlete. We hear it from others all the time but don't ever believe we will be in that position in our own lives. We were taught to say no and achieve the goal. Well, here I was, a football player, but only on my resume. I had to start from the lowest bottom of the workforce totem pole. I didn't even know where that starting line was.

I did odd jobs trying to make ends meet. I had been a hard worker my entire life, so I just needed to apply that to my new life. I tried to find something, not necessarily as a career per se, but something where I could earn a lot of money.

I had a lot of education, although I was not a graduate with a degree. However, I had been in college for four years, so I was able to put that on my resume, along with being in sports. I highlighted discipline and teamwork, things that companies look for outside the workplace that would give me an edge over other candidates, and I emphasized those in my qualifications.

I finally went to a temp agency and was given an assignment at a timeshare company. It was a well-paying office job that gave me weekends off to be with Tyler and hours that allowed me to drop him off and pick him up from school. It was really soft collections, not anything where I was yelling or had to be hardcore with individuals to request payment. The job came naturally to me, and it wasn't long before I demonstrated success by bringing in large amounts from the long-standing accounts the company had trouble collecting on. I believe that was due to my being able to talk well from the representation events that I did as an athlete, the press conferences from sports, and what I learned in my youth being involved in the church.

After my temporary probation period, I was hired full-time, and I was so happy to begin to make a small salary.

One day, our director approached me and pulled me into her office to discuss with me her appreciation for a job well done, and she asked what my plans were for the future.

I did not know, so she discussed my potential for a position in sales. At the time, I didn't want to be a salesman. I had this picture of the people who came and knocked on doors, and those doors got slammed right back into their faces. That would be too much rejection for me.

She discussed the role from a different perspective. She explained business to business (B2B) sales with me, and as I thought about it, it made some sense to me. I also knew that sales carried with it great commission opportunities and extra money.

The director continued that she was thinking of opening a new account executive position and asked if I would think about it and that she would mentor me. This side of the business within the company had promise, and it was growing fast.

This director became my mentor and coach. The department was on the move and making money. I was making money. Under her guidance, I developed a keen business acumen and learned how to discuss and negotiate deals.

I was still raw from the loss of my life's dream, but I began to trade in my sports cleats for business suits. One day that turned my entire career around was when my mentor took us on a department field trip, and we went to the Honda Center in Anaheim, CA.

That was my first experience going to see a corporate speaker live. It was Zig Ziglar. It was sold out, with about 20,000 people in the building. I had never heard of him, but he is considered to be one of the best in our field of all time, "the GOAT" in today's vernacular. He also professed his faith in God.

Ziglar changed my entire selling career. While I did well at building rapport and speaking with groups or individuals, there was one gem of advice he gave that still sticks with me today:

"Sell with integrity, never lie, and you will be successful. Don't persuade people into buying anything."

My mentor asked me what I learned that day, and I shared the highlights, but that right there aligned with my faith and upbringing in the Word of God and made sense to me. Something clicked.

Salesmen are usually considered exaggerators, liars, and manipulators. I wanted to be different. I wanted to serve, bring value, and help others through the products that I chose to sell. I vowed never to sell someone anything that didn't deliver a benefit to them.

I would never lie to my consumers, ever. If they wanted to know the price, I would tell them. Whatever they asked, I would accommodate truthfully and honestly.

From that day forward, I doubled my salary, and I was happy with the skills that came with that success. It was almost like becoming an All-American in the corporate world.

I was receiving praise for my efforts; I was winning again, receiving extra benefits for my achievements.

That feeling was reminiscent of those good ole days on the football field. So, in a way, it took the place of what I felt I lost in football.

The department added more roles, and our staff grew in title responsibility. I had gone from small-time collections to a new business coordinator, which included traveling around the country and speaking to top executives around the world. I brought a unique perspective that had not been exemplified in this arena before with my experience from participation in Division 1 and professional sports.

My motivation was my faith and fatherhood. Not much caught me off guard, and I was determined to be a student of my industry and learn as much as I could. I had goals. I believed that I could become the president of a company someday. I knew experience was key.

My life was back on track. At least I felt happy to be moving in a direction that would still enable me to see my hopes and dreams come to fruition financially. I desired to get married and have a family, not just for me but for Tyler as well.

After about three years in my new role, I met someone. We got engaged, and a year after I proposed, we married, and I became a father to the son she had before we met.

My second son, Kellen M. Crayton, was born into this union and added such a blessing to my family. He is ten years younger than Tyler, and I felt more mature and experienced this go around as a father.

Kellen's mother and I were married for about four years. It is always a very difficult thing to go through a divorce, and there are things I know we both regret. I never wanted to get a divorce because my family was so against it. Plus, I witnessed others in my family celebrating years of being together and I strongly desired to experience the same, and I think I stayed as long as I did because of that. That is not something that I feel is the best, but it is a real thing of being too loyal to a cause. In the end, we did not fight or allow it to get ugly; we amicably decided to go our separate ways. Nonetheless, the one thing that I had going was that my career was taking off. I had been with my company for about six years, and I was thriving.

Section 3:
The Trials and the Evil of Days

"The ultimate tragedy is not the oppression and cruelty by the bad people but the silence over that by the good people."

—Dr. Martin Luther King Jr.

CHAPTER 7

When Tragedy Strikes

My family has seen its share of sickness, injuries, broken bones, and bruising before. There are times we actually felt we were invincible because we always know we are covered by Christ's protection, but this time, it hit differently when I got the news to meet my family at the hospital.

It was a normal day on July 6, 2006. I got up, did my normal routine at work, and at about nine something, while sitting at my desk, my brother Chris called me and told me I needed to get to the hospital ASAP. I asked what happened, and he said, "It's Garrett, just come." I told my supervisor that I had to get to the hospital for some type of emergency, and I jumped in my car. The hospital was about twenty-five minutes from my workplace, and for some reason, my spirit was not sitting easy on the drive. It's almost as if I knew this was more than just getting to the hospital for a minor situation, and in my spirit, I felt like something terrible had happened. The feeling was so deep in my stomach that out of nowhere, I began to cry all the way there, even before I knew what to cry about. I just had a feeling that my buddy, my brother, was gone.

However, then, my mind vacillated to the other extreme to have faith and be positive until I received confirmation, so I just kept driving. My hands acted as wipers along the way.

As soon as I arrived, I made a beeline for the information desk. There were two older women sitting there, and before I could utter a word, they pointed to me and said, "He is on the second floor," and gave me the room and ICU number. I knew our familial resemblance was striking, but I didn't expect them to know where to direct me purely on sight. I made my way to the floor, and immediately, I saw my younger sister Nicki down the hall. The distance in my mind was equal to that of an NFL football field, and it seemed like it would take me forever to get to the end zone. Nicki was crying, bawling rather. So, I picked up the pace and made a mad dash toward her and arrived at a set of glass doors. There he lay, his body lifeless. My mom and dad were over to the side with the nurse. I could hear them make my introduction to the nurse. My mom said, "That's Garrett's younger brother."

I can't explain it, but I didn't even have words for it. It was my big brother, Garrett, "G'Money," my QB, just lying there. I felt like shaking my body to wake up, but this was real. He had the shoes that I gave him signed by Chris Webber, the basketball player. I remember standing over him and just looking over his body for probably about ten minutes. I could do nothing but stand over him.

More and more of us started coming in one by one. The double glass doors were more like revolving doors going from open to shut to open again. Shortly thereafter, Letrice and my brother-in-law Terron arrived, and I remember vividly Letrice banging on the glass doors in pain. Then Chris arrived.

For the purpose of the privacy of our thoughts together, I will not share that intimate time that we all had over Garrett's body. It became too much for Letrice as she was the closest in age to Garrett. We all were very close, but Garrett and Letrice's bond was super tight. They are only two years apart. Letrice is as tough as they come, but she had to step out for a while. My dad left the room because his best friend, who was with them when they were on the golf course where my brother would take his last breath, began to console him.

I was still in utter disbelief, and I had difficulty accepting this reality. So, as we had been taught for so long to pray, Chris, Terron, and I began to pray for Garrett, and when I say pray, I mean praying like Jesus in the Garden of Gethsemane, praying so hard that we would sweat blood if we had to. That is how hard we went into joining our faith together to bring him back from the dead. We all really believed that. All the stories we read in the Bible, Lazarus, the Holy Spirit's working power, all that, we knew it could happen, and we wanted it to happen for us.

We prayed in tongues. I don't know for how long, but we believed that our prayers were going to move the miracle-working power of God, so we prayed louder and harder.

We saw his foot moving, and I blurted out, "It's working!" because when we touched his hands, he was still warm. But right then, my mom brought to our attention that we had been praying so hard that we were the ones shaking and moving the bed, and his foot movement was created by us.

My mom, who was just sitting in the corner while we were praying, asked us to stop. She said to us, "Boys, he is gone, and you know what? He will not come back. And you guys shouldn't want him to come back because he is in paradise with God."

So, I walked toward the private grieving room where I had first seen Nikki. It was a short walk, but it felt like I had traveled for miles. Garrett had passed in my father's arms, so I couldn't imagine what was going on with my father, who is our family rock and Superman. The wisest and strongest man I know, just crippled and sitting on the bench in the room. This would be the first time I ever saw my dad cry.

It wasn't a "Why, God?" kind of cry, but one born out of sheer shock, and I had never ever seen him devastated.

During this tender moment, it was just me, Chris, and my dad, so I stopped what I was doing, and we began to console our father. We lost a brother; he lost a son. Is this what God felt when he witnessed the death of our Lord? Our earthly father was crying out to his Heavenly Father not just because He was *God* but because *God* knew personally what angst and heartache my dad was going through.

Along with us in the room was my dad's closest friend. Chris and I guarded the door as other close relatives began to arrive. It just wasn't the time to talk to my father, so we did what we could to protect others from coming in at the door. After hours of our huge family coming in one by one, we collected ourselves because we now had to go inform our children, as they all were in school. I left to pick up the kids, and as I was on my way, it hit me. How was I going to tell Tyler? If our lives were an intricately decorated family room table, Garrett was the centerpiece. Especially for his nieces and nephews, he was the life of the party. There were countless days and weekends at his home for game night.

We had been at the hospital so long, and we finally made our way back to my parents' house so that we all could grieve together privately as word of Garrett's death spread fast. When we got to the house, it was just family there. I'm sure people wanted to come through, but we all were just trying to recover.

I called a couple of my friends, but after that, I just couldn't and didn't answer the phone for three days. I didn't move off the couch for three days. I just lay there in a fetal position with my back to the world around me. I didn't even turn on the TV.

I would hear the kids leave for school and when they came back in the door. I would turn around to chat briefly, but all I wanted to do was just sleep. I had cried and was so fatigued mentally and emotionally.

I was still living with my ex when this tragedy happened. We were only separated at the time and were still working on the divorce settlement so that it would be finalized. My other siblings were able to deal with their feelings accompanied by their spouses, but I just fought through it alone at home. The tragedy did not bring us back together in any way.

It was time for the funeral and the wake. Again, we took turns going back and forth, consoling each other, trying to articulate how we got to this and saying our last goodbyes. We all stood over Garrett's casket, huddled up, our arms all tied together. Then my dad said, "I don't want you guys to ever stress in your life ever again, not about one thing!" That is what I remember my dad saying. He went on to tell us, "Don't let the minor things in life like stress be the difference in you fulfilling God's promise. Stress can kill you!"

His words ran through my entire being, and as I thought about my life in the context of his advice, I determined that I would never stress again. It was then and there that I decided to not work a job that I did not have a passion for; I was not going to chase the things of this world.

The dynamics of our lives changed. I changed. I remember when our family used to love being in the second row, being known as the First Family, but now we all became so introverted, and during this time of bereavement and mourning, none of us wanted to be upfront.

Before I knew it, sitting in the back of the church became the new normal. There were times I didn't want to be there, but we wanted to be there for my dad.

About a week later, I began to get separation anxiety. I was missing my brother. To add salt to that wound, I had to process my divorce and not be able to see my son every day.

My soon-to-be ex-wife and I were doing this visitation arrangement that would allow us to work out a great way to spend as much time with Kellen as we both could. It wasn't an easy discussion with my brother's death, but I still had to work out Kellen's situation with her. He was only one year old, and she did not make it easy. Everybody else had somebody to grieve with. I didn't, so it was just me and my boys that I could lean on.

At times like this, people mean well when they tell you they will be there for you. As the days turned into weeks, the crowd dissipated. Those who remained were my very closest friends. Terry, in particular, who was there at the start going through it with me, helped me to deal with the void of not having the spousal support that was left with the loss of Garrett, and he still does to this day.

I had to decide how to move on, not just forward but in a way that would honor Garret and make him proud. For one, I wouldn't chase titles anymore.

I had to try to process how I was going to begin to move forward with my life. I had to stop thinking about making money and titles and start to look at my life from a different perspective.

I knew I needed to change my relationship with God because I definitely wasn't living right...all the way.

About two weeks after the funeral, I was standing outside my parents' house because my family and I all stuck together for the next months and year.

I went outside to look over the hills, and my mom came outside while I silently cried, streams of tears just running down my face. She came over next to me and just put her head on my shoulder. We were side by side looking at the mountains, and I said aloud what I was thinking in my heart, "I'm missing Garrett so much."

She replied quietly and said, "I do, too." And we just stood there for about ten minutes looking over the sunset of the mountains. She put her arm around me, and I put mine around her.

I may not have been physically bruised, but I had internal bleeding from the emotional bruising. My heart was broken.

Somehow, I knew that nothing would ever break me like that ever again. Not my divorce, my troubles from the past, living in the present, or my future. I am dedicating my life to making sure the things Garrett taught me will never be in vain.

It was a process. One second, I was okay, then other times, my mind would seesaw between memories of Garrett and thoughts of my own mortality.

CHAPTER 8

Anointed in the Middle

One vow and promise I made to myself was to never be unhappy again, and I decided that monetary things were not going to be a factor in my decisions going forward. No matter the title or position, I was going to do something I loved.

My brother's death really made me look inward and upward with my eyes on where I would spend eternity. I began to get back on track, making my relationship with Christ the first thing. I knew my life needed this change.

I didn't know what specifically needed to change, but I knew that I wasn't living one hundred percent for God. Even with being involved in church all my life, I didn't know what it meant to have the pure one-on-one relationship I witnessed in the lives of my parents.

I looked at my life as a father and provider and contemplated the legacy I would leave on this earth. Was I even really happy with my life? Was it all about me or did I really want to do God's plan?

I left the job that I was working at when Garrett had passed and started to look for work that involved sports, but before I finally got to making the move to look for a sport-related career position, I worked for some of the top best hotels, most notably at the world-famous Hilton Del Mar.

In this short span, I learned a lot about the business of service, hospitality, and tour sites, which would bode well for me in the future. This was a unique experience in my life.

I was still not fulfilled with what I felt was my passion, as getting back into sports was my heart's passion. Somehow, I wanted to land a job in the field of athletics. I went to job fair after job fair until a longtime family friend was able to get me registered for a job fair held on the Marine Corps base at Camp Pendleton. Now that I had so many years of sales, hospitality, and services experience on my resume, I thought I could find a good fit for a new, promising direction and career growth.

I was dressed to the nines now that I had my teeth in the game. If there is one thing that I enjoyed, it was being distinguished from others in my personal style.

I am a traditional suit guy, but I like it tailored to my body, similar to that of the James Bond 007 persona.

I had my suit, my briefcase, and my resume. Time had passed, lessons were learned, and now I stood a different man, seasoned with experience and validated by a confidence in the overcoming spirit that was in the two-year-old boy who ran around that high school track to the amazement of his parents. I also had the mindset of changing my life as I still carried the thoughts of living my life the way Garrett would.

I was approached by a representative of 24Hour Fitness. He was donned in his logo polo shirt and seemed to just assume I was interested. Even though I indulged him, I knew that I didn't want to be a trainer or a sales manager. Nonetheless, I had come to never miss an opportunity to learn, listen, and leverage information, so I followed him over to the table.

I inquired of him about what position they were looking to fill. He answered that they were looking for club managers.

Now, the next natural progression was about salary, and after he led with six-figures, all I needed to know next was where to sign up!

He quickly brought me over to speak to the HR representative who was there that day, and after a short conversation, they were both impressed and gave me more detailed information about the position. They explained that they were thinking outside the box as they would normally fill this role from within but wanted to open up managerial positions to outside talent.

They were calling it the CMT program (Club Manager Trainee). They later got in touch with me, and we set up an interview. Again, I dressed to impress...which over time became my calling card, and soon, I was sitting out in front of the corporate office that is attached to one of their main facilities.

I checked in, and I waited, waited, and waited. I watched employees come in and out for three hours as they repeatedly updated me that a meeting with the VP was running late.

I would normally get an attitude and think, *Why should I wait for them?* But internally, something gave me the patience to just sit and wait. At the third hour, a man came down in sweats...Oklahoma Sooner sweats at that. He apologized and said, "I didn't even know you were still down here. You waited all that time?"

I said, "Yes." He brought me into the main room, and we discussed the opportunity.

I was honest with him about my experience in this industry. He stated something that has stuck with me to this day. He said, "I looked at your resume and took notice of your sports career, along with your experience and hobbies." In particular, he took note of my coaching youth sports and church volunteer work. He continued, "We are looking for people like you. I saw not the experience but your discipline as an athlete. My son is on scholarship as a wrestler at the University of Oklahoma, and when I saw that rival Nebraska national champion that you put on your resume, I knew I needed to meet you." That was a great accomplishment.

Furthermore, he said, "I can teach you the business side of how to run your own club. What I can't teach," he added, "is will, discipline, and effort." These were qualities that he saw in me both on paper and in our interaction—qualities that were developed through the battles on and off the field and the bruises to my body, emotions, and ego when things didn't appear to go my way.

It felt like a page right out of the book of Romans. You've probably heard this very popular verse: "And we know that all things work together for good to those who love God, to those who are called according to *His* purpose" (Romans 8:28, NKJV).

God was making all the hard work work for my good. They hired me as the first-ever CMT, which was epic! This is a company that is known worldwide, and by His grace, God allowed me this unique blessing.

The team was on my shoulders again. I was really passionate about helping people get healthy. I believed in the company's mission, and the role paid very well. While I knew my years of hospitality and service background would go a long way in this environment, I could hear Zig Ziglar in my ears reminding me about integrity in sales. I was ready to put everything I had learned along the way into practice. The salary was a great incentive, but the integrity of the Crayton name, Garrett's legacy, and the legacy I wanted for my sons were the real motivators.

I did my best to understand the playbook of the company; the rules, the expectations of bringing in a profit and breaking down where the opportunities were and knowing what to look for to make my business successful were something I just dived into like the offensive and defensive playbooks in my past.

I had learned from my previous experiences that it takes time and a plan. I was coachable and had follow-through. My hustle and tenacious attitude grew stronger, but I needed to learn more. I never really struggled to grasp information, but I was focused on working with the expectations of learning my new craft.

Suddenly, ten days after I was hired, there was a club opening, and they let me know that I had to be ready when one opened. I had no idea what I was doing; I didn't even know the producers of the club yet. What I did have experience with was having integrity and tapping into the skills and knowledge of my teammates until I knew how to execute the responsibilities of my new role. Being with 24 Hour Fitness really grew me and my business acumen. I grew as a leader, I was a success as the first CMT, and I was the poster boy for the new system. I won so many service, sales, and leadership awards and grew into a mentor for other new and experienced club managers. I was an entire success story for the 24 Hour Fitness brand.

There was still something inside of me that I felt was undone, and that was being in a true sports organization, being part of a professional team. What I had to decide was whether I was willing to give up my salary to chase my dream.

I did some serious research on what potential changes could occur in my life. Mainly, I needed to consider what impact it would have on my sons. At the time, I lived in a community that had the best school systems for the boys. I would sacrifice anything to make sure that they were good first.

My faith in God was growing, so I was developing more faith. I knew that He led me to the 24 Hour Fitness job, and I was being blessed throughout my entire career. I did things the right way, and people knew that my life was consistent with my faith. I didn't preach with words; I did it through my actions. I ran my clubs my way, and all those in contact with me knew God was a true force in my life.

So, if I was going to make this jump, I was letting God direct my path and working on my faith when it came to having complete trust in Him. If the door was going to be open for me, I asked God to do so. He did. I applied for several positions, including a small position in third-party ticket sales with the Los Angeles Chargers.

The position involved making one hundred and forty calls all day long trying to get people to buy season tickets, a process that I hadn't done since I first retired from football over twenty years before. What made this job harder was that the Chargers had just relocated from San Diego to LA.

The most difficult aspect of the job was that I would have to take a $90,000 pay cut if I accepted the role. Yes, you read it right...$90,000. The job didn't guarantee that the Chargers would hire the best sellers. It would just give me access to get in front of them.

I was going on forty years of age, starting over, and in competition with other applicants and coworkers whose ages averaged around twenty-three years old...all fresh out of college, with sports industry degrees, and wanting to work their way up to having the sports career I had attained at my age.

One thing was for sure: this was going to be new territory, but I had mastered the art of "beginning again," and I got my mind ready to take on another challenge. Smile and dial was the mantra.

I remember going to my kids, sitting them down and asking their thoughts. I really wanted to show them that first, we would make a family decision for us all to go after our passions, and I wanted them to be a part of this journey with me, and they were going to be a part of some of the sacrifices that were about to be made. I told them I was looking at taking a chance at doing this new path in my life. I believed in myself and God that I could quickly move up if I put in this hard work, but I wouldn't be bringing in the money that I used to, so we all would have to sacrifice. I wouldn't be able to buy the shoes, the gear, and the video games on demand.

My boys said, "Pops, you have done everything for us. Go get what you want! We are behind you!"

So, I decided to go for it and went through the interview process. They offered me the position. I had so many emotions that first day when I pulled up to the Chargers facility. I quickly processed the joy and the reflections of my journey to get to this moment and that this was Garrett's favorite team, so I looked up to the sky before I entered the double doors where they had a large bolt symbol and said underneath my breath, "Here we go, brother, run through the end zone." I knew the hard work was ahead of me that came with a decrease in salary, but I trusted God and I knew over the years of committing to my relationship with Him, I was going to be okay.

I came to accept that if I was not going to play in the NFL, then why not take my talents to the corporate side—twenty-five years later? In every role that I had from the time I began my journey in business sales, I wanted to set myself apart and remember that one way I stood out was in my attire.

I wanted to be unique and stand out in this industry and also represent my culture, so I decided to learn how to tie a bow tie. This may seem insignificant to discuss, but I thought it would help me stand out, and everyone needs a trademark look, so the bow tie was going to be mine. It was classy, and also it would make a statement because not a lot of people tie their own bow tie. I was in a no-clip-on frame of mind.

Since I came in with God confidence, I quickly shot up the sales charts and became the number one employee when it came to ticket sales. I was still struggling with my personal finances, as the low income was eating up all the savings I had. I was not bringing in my normal salary and commission I had been accustomed to for the last ten-plus years, so I had to make another decision to downsize my living arrangements. I went from a condo to a studio apartment. We went from a full-spread choice of food to what I could afford. The boys slept in the only room, while I slept in the living room on the couch. This would be my bedroom for about two years until I was able to climb in my responsibilities and increase my finances with the Chargers. It was pressing and stressful at times, but I also knew it was temporary, and it really stretched my faith.

One day, I got an email from one of the top executives' assistants to come to his office. I came into the office not knowing what the conversation would entail, but I knew I had done nothing that would require discipline, so I walked into the office with an open mind. We greeted one another as always, and after some small talk, he began to praise me for my quick contributions. He shared that the organization had been recognizing the hard work I put in, and they also knew my struggles, along with my goals to stay and move up with the organization. He said that they would be honored to continue to keep me as a valued employee. The real reason for the meeting was to inform me that they found a way to open up a position for me, so I got the promotion that I needed to start to survive again. After a year, I was able to not only get back to my salary range but had the opportunity to make more. With the new role I now had the ability to level up and move up with a bigger role as a part of the executive team and the executive side of the organization. I wanted to give a big "Let's goooo" to God, but I played it professionally. I witnessed the work of God and how He works behind the scenes, which again strengthened my confidence in Him. The experience confirmed that He keeps His promises of making sure we know that He was doing that work I couldn't see. My new role title was "Manager of Premium Experiences." This role is a crucial part of the lifeline of any sports team's business.

With my experience and savviness that I learned in jobs past, I was confident that I could be an intricate part of the success of growing the company's clientele as needed, so I began to handle the top clients for the LA Chargers.

I made tremendous contacts with the biggest companies in the world. The NFL is the biggest brand in the world. It was amazing, and I felt on top again. I had access to the entire stadium.

My relationships inside the organization grew, and I began to establish relationships with the owner, the coaches, and the players in the NFL. They became family. I was living life as a business executive and using my mind instead of banging my body in the NFL. I knew this was what I was finally called to do and where I needed to be. This was my heart's desire, and it was God who put me on top again after all I had endured. This was the pinnacle of my life. I am ready to enjoy the good life and the fruits of my labor.

A couple of seasons had passed, and I just kept thriving and thriving with the organization. I had moved out of the small studio apartment and moved into a bigger space, and the kids and I began to live back in the world of no more lack and sacrifice.

One day at work, our office executive director at our owner's office asked me if I would be open to participating in being part of the organization's first-ever diversity meeting. The meeting would consist of five individuals who had beaten the odds and stigma of employees in the sports industry. The diversity panel included a Mexican-American woman representing the Latino community, another woman who was the first female trainer in the NFL, and last was a prominent executive female figure in our organization who had been with the ownership team for about thirty years.

The interview would be conducted by our female media guru, as she was the team's sports anchor. The meeting would be on March 9, 2020. I immediately said yes, and I was so enthusiastic about the opportunity. It was an honor to be asked and recognized because, in my profession, it was especially unique that someone my age had gone so far so quickly. I was forty-three years of age and worked my way up from the mailroom to the executive suites in a matter of six months, and they wanted me to tell my story.

I remember having a new VP of sales, and just like with a new coach, he initially wanted to bring in his own guys for the role I had, but with the favor of God, he couldn't negate that I was very good at what I was doing and my results caused me to stand apart from the rest.

Also, my character and integrity were never questioned; I always followed procedure; I was never late to a day or to meetings; and at the right times, I always proclaimed, "I am a Christian."

I didn't blast the Jesus freak phrase, but I did represent Him in my spirit everywhere I went. As part of my inner work, I would bring my copy of a best-selling Christian daily devotional to work with me as part of my daily Bible study. I would get to work early before others arrived and immerse myself in it, highlighting the nuggets I would uncover.

After a while, my teammates would stop by to ask what book was on my desk. Those inquiries turned into full-blown Bible questions.

My team thought it would be cool if I sent some encouraging words each morning and developed a group chat. At first, I was reluctant, but I took on the responsibility to be obedient and sent out a text after I read my passage each business day from that point to the end of the year, which was six months. I did this and shared via a group text, and word got out about what I was doing, so more and more team members joined the group. It became kind of a small Bible study with those who were interested.

This was something that tested my discipline and growth for myself to be able to share my passion for helping others grow or find a relationship with God. "We do it all together" is what I told each person, sorta like a QB.

I was consistent and completed that task, and I did it for the six months that I promised.

March 9 had come for the diversity meeting, and I didn't want to miss this opportunity to represent myself in the best light, so I woke up early to prepare. When I woke up, I felt an unusual pain in my shoulder, and I could feel myself starting to get a headache, but I refused to let anything stand in the way of this event. It was too important.

I knew it would be in front of my peers, but I had no idea that it would be held in the football team's meeting room in the presence of the entire office staff, and the Chargers head coach and staff! It seemed that everyone was there!

I was at the end of the table, and we went in order from right to left. I would be the last to speak and anchor the panel. I told my story, and the people were so amazed by the testimony of my life. In the end, most of them approached me with compliments on my speaking ability and, more importantly, on how my story resonated and impacted them.

The next day, I had an appointment to meet with my mentor from 24 Hour Fitness. We met at one of my favorite restaurants in the city, so the commute that day was easy as we both lived close by. I woke up again, and I felt progressively worse. We did meet, but I didn't feel well, so we ended the meeting much earlier than anticipated.

Then, about twenty-four hours later, I was sick and feeling a lot of discomfort in my arm! What I was about to endure, I wouldn't wish on anyone, not even the worst of my enemies.

CHAPTER 9

Silence in the Face of Injustice

Samson is one of my favorite characters in the Bible, and I sometimes liken myself to him in that as small and frail as I looked, my body was strong.

I may have been 155 to 160 pounds soaking wet, but my bone structure was made in such a way that others would describe being hit by me on the field as akin to being hit by a Mack truck! I could run people over, and they just couldn't understand it.

But, in 2020, while adjusting to the "new normal" that the COVID-19 virus created for the world as we knew it, my body began to fail me for a whole different reason. I took care of my body and never really had issues.

I knew I had to find out the root cause. I was able to walk around, but I had gotten really weak, and I was desperately trying to figure out what was happening to me. I was unable to move my right arm as it became too stiff to move, and I began to develop some abnormal growth from the bottom of my jaw to my chest. In one week, the growth on my neck was disfigured, and I developed a large tumor-like growth half the size of a tennis ball on the side of my neck, so I felt it was time to go to the hospital.

Right when I got there, they sent me straight to the ICU, and I was admitted immediately because they could see that something wasn't right. Since it was the beginning of COVID-19 and the pandemic, no one besides administered patients was allowed in the hospital. They told me to call my dad, who was waiting in the parking lot, and tell him that I was going to be there for a while and they needed to run more tests.

That was our starting point. When checking all my vital signs, they asked several important questions, and I answered them. I do remember them asking about some dental questions, but the main thing for me was that I felt my body failing me. I recalled a visit a year prior where I told my dentist during my cleanings about pain in the right side of my mouth, but it went unaddressed.

Still, that was the least of my worries at that point in time. I had lost a lot of weight, and my pain was just getting worse. After the test results, they escorted me back to the ICU, and soon enough, the doctor came in to share my results. The neurosurgeon had consulted with an infectious disease doctor who confirmed that the right side of my mouth was the source of a rare infection that required next-day surgery, and they needed to make preparations immediately. When they would ask me what my pain level was at between one and ten, I would say twelve; that is how much pain I was in. Medication and sedation were needed day and night to help with the constant pain. My condition required two surgeons: one for my shoulder area, which was completely locked into place, and the other for my neck, which was enlarged.

The plan was multiple surgeries in hopes that they could strip my body of the infection in an effort to avoid organ failure. I was too tired to talk, so the doctor would FaceTime my parents to keep them updated on my progress.

I was prepped and readied for the first of a possible four to seven scheduled surgeries. Every other day, they were going to try and get the infection. I would have to wear a wound vacuum that was strapped to my chest. A wound vacuum is a device that has a tube that sucks the infection, pus, and blood out of the body, and it goes into a large spare tank gas bucket. It ran from the large incision at the top of my chest to the bucket. It had to stay connected to my body at all times. I was bed-stricken twenty-four hours a day; I couldn't shower and couldn't get up to use the restroom either. I had to urinate in a urine bottle that was strapped to my hospital bed.

I admitted myself on March 17, and my first surgery was on March 22. I had survived the first surgery. The second surgery would be on my birthday, which was March 24. When preparing me for surgery again, upon verification, they noticed it was my birthday. When I got wheeled into the surgical room, as they were strapping me in under the surgical lights, they asked if today was my birthday. I said yes, and the surgery team said, "Happy birthday." And before they put me under, they all promised me that they would make sure I woke up. These are things you just never think about, that I could actually die while under the knife. When I woke up in my room, there was a note card from the entire ICU team signed with a birthday card. I still have that card, and it still brings out in me the emotion of gratitude of that day.

I was so tired every day that I barely had time to talk with my parents. My energy level was so depleted. It was time for the third surgery, and I went through the same process, not knowing if I would wake up on Earth or in heaven. After the third surgery, I woke up and was just thanking God that I was still alive. I could feel my body losing its strength, which was difficult because I was an athlete, and my body had always had its strength.

Sometime during that day, I looked outside the window, and I stated to God that if He allowed me to live through this, I would walk whatever path that He wanted. To be honest, I actually wasn't afraid of dying because of the choices I made to do what was right before this evil day came and when Garrett passed. I really did deepen my Christian walk. I knew for a fact eternity was promised to me, but I didn't want to go yet. I thought about my boys and being there for them as they grew up to be men. Kellen was almost set to graduate, and Tyler was in college. I want to see them get married and play with my grandkids, so I made another decree to God that I would walk in His desire no matter what.

Here we went again, setting up for what would be my fourth surgery in seven days. My body was frail, and I didn't know if I would survive another surgery. Right before they were going to take me to the surgical room, the doctor ordered an MRI to see how much of the infection was left. When the results came back this time, the infection was completely gone. So, they canceled the surgery. The first thing that I did was FaceTime my parents and the doctor, and I got to give my parents the news. The one thing that I will never forget was as the doctor began to walk out of the room to give me and my parents some privacy, I looked at my doctor and said, "Doc, thank you for saving my life!" His response was, "It was my honor." That sent me into such an emotional cry. Doctors know the real deal, and that statement from him let me know that he fought for me to live. Although I knew it was going to be a long, long recovery, I just relished in the moment with my parents and the knowledge that I was going to remain on this earth. I praised God all night in between rests. It took me the next two or three weeks to get better, and with physical therapy, refueling my body, and following their personalized plan, I was able to go home. Since I was bedstricken for a month or so, I had to relearn how to walk, and my arm still was immobile. I still had the wound vacuum strapped to my chest while I rehabbed. Before I left home, I would have to clear two series of tests. One was putting a PICC IV in my bicep to my heart that would protect and strengthen my heart from the infection spread, and the other was the wound vacuum test that would consist of me having to change my bandages every other day without pain medicine.

The wound vacuum test had to be done by a special care nurse every other day. The main reason for the test was that they had to make sure I could withstand the insurmountable pain that came with changing the bandages and gauze that was inserted into the skeleton system of my collarbone with each cleaning. Envision the board game Operation, where you have to get the bone out without touching the edges with some small medical tweezers, and if you touch the edge of the board, the nose lights up, and the board shakes and buzzes, signifying you lost. Well, this was not the game; it was real life. Touching flesh burns. It burned beyond anything I have ever felt, and it will make any person wail and gnash their teeth. The pain is indescribable.

My first thought in hindsight was that I could not believe that Jesus died for us in so much pain on the cross. This was nothing compared to what He endured on the cross. There is no way I could ever go through His pain on the cross.

I barely passed all the tests. It took sheer will and mindset only because I really wanted to go home. I was finally discharged after six weeks. I came into the hospital at approximately 200 pounds, and I left at a fragile 148 pounds, smaller than I was when I entered my freshman year of high school. My parents could barely recognize me. I also had so many instructions for my PICC IV and a special ordered wound vacuum that had to stay attached to me. I was required to have twenty-four-hour nurse care, so I would have to leave my permanent residence and stay with my parents for the unforeseeable future. The doctor said that the average recovery time could be three to five years or longer, but the first year was the most important because my physical body would never be one hundred percent again.

The meaning of rehabilitation is "the action of restoring something that has been damaged to its former condition, and the action of restoring someone to former privileges or reputation after a period of disfavor." In short, it helps someone to try to live a normal life again. As an athlete, I know what treatment and rehab therapy are when it comes to an injury. You can just put your ankle on ice, and in two days or a week, you are able to work through some pain and discomfort. Recovering from a serious life-threatening illness is a totally different ball game.

The list of rehabilitation therapy treatments:

1. Wound vacuum treatment, three days a week
2. Every day at 11 a.m., injections into my heart for twenty minutes
3. Arm physical therapy, one hour every Tuesday and Thursday
4. Chronic & PTSD therapy
5. Multiple doctor visits

These were just a few adjustments that I would have to endure. COVID-19 was very new, and it was still such a threat to people who had underlying conditions, so since I was at such high risk, I couldn't have anyone visit me while I rehabbed at home. My two boys couldn't even come by due to my open wound. The symptoms of severe sweats, nightmares, and other internal opposition began to bombard my mind. I didn't know how to deal with the physical pain, the change to my body, trying to adjust to the disability because I couldn't use my golden arm. The pain management from the first rehab was a pain level of ten, and that would last up to eight to twelve weeks. The next phase would be trying to regain the strength in my body, which is an ongoing process that I still have challenges with to this day. I had to deal with Bell's palsy, which is a side effect that came after the infection, due to the stress that it put on my brain. I went through a brain tumor scare, scars began to form on my body, and the battles continue to go on within, the inside side effects that I can't see. There were many adjustments to many things, and I got to the point that I was going to have to fight to get back to some type of normalcy.

The question to myself was, "What am I going to do now?" I couldn't work at this time as I was on disability. I had lost my ability to do what I loved again because of my physical ailments, like not being able to lift more than 10 pounds, blurred vision, fatigue, etc. My ability to work in sports was limited again. So, what was I going to do?

I went to the prayer room, as that was the only area in my life that I had faith in.

I went to a therapist to discuss all the mental health troubles that were making me depressed, having nightmares about the surgeries, the mental and physical attacks. The therapy helped; not only was I able to talk with my God, but it also helped me to speak with a physical person. I knew I needed to keep myself busy, so I decided in 2021 that I would go back and finish my degree at Pitt. I only had two more classes to finish my Social Science degree, so I thought this would be a really good time to possibly finish. I called to enroll myself back in school, and I was determined to make sure that I finished this time. I wanted a degree. God began to show me, and although I was not one hundred percent sure what direction He wanted me to go in, I had faith, and I declared I would follow His direction when I was in the hospital bed, so I felt going back to school was going to be beginning to strengthen my patience and my trust in Him.

When I called to enroll, the academic center stated that my major in which I had all my credits was no longer available, and I would have to change my major. I would have to decide on a new major. After opening up, being honest and vulnerable with my advisor about what had transpired with my life and what I knew that God was putting on my heart, she suggested the thought of me going to law school.

I thought, *Law?* That is something I would have never chosen, but my heart was open to new possibilities, and after prayer, I said okay. I wrote a special note to the athletic director and the contacts that I still had there, and they showed me favor. I received a letter saying that if I completed the ten required classes in a year, they would pay for my classes. I would have to take four classes in the summer and five in the fall (ten classes in seven months). I knew I had to be disciplined and focused, and I made up my mind that I would study so hard that I wouldn't let this opportunity pass again. I was going to have to juggle rehab, my mental health, and pain management to get through this, as I was still only in year two of rehabilitation.

I started my summer session load of classes and instantly fell in love with law. It did so much for me because maybe I didn't give myself enough credit for being as smart because I was best known for being an athlete.

I was dealing with billion-dollar companies, and because my colleagues all had degrees, and I didn't have my degree, I felt less than. This was an area in my life where I allowed the enemy to continue his attacks on my self-esteem. I took this opportunity to grow, and it is not easy to understand and study law if you are not serious about it. A lot of work went into my studies, and I wanted to make sure that I appreciated Pitt so much that I didn't want to be average. I wanted to show them my appreciation and get the best grades possible, straight A's. That mindset strengthened me, and in one year, I received my law degree. Not only did I receive a college degree, but I maintained my highest GPA of 3.8, one grade from straight A's, the highest average of my life. A true heart desire of mine was to be a University of Pittsburgh alum, not just a football alum. God's plan was beginning to come into place.

During the time of getting my degree, I began to learn the ability to write. I relied on my speaking talent, but my writing skills needed a lot of work when it came to term papers, and the work I needed to put in would strengthen my new ability to research and gain wisdom and knowledge through studying. I believe God used this time to show me that speaking His Word requires the right studying habits, understanding comes through research, and God's laws and ways need to be read and then recited through words and deeds.

My family watched as I worked day and night to obtain my law degree through all the distressful ailments I was going through. After thirty years, I had finally obtained something that in my heart meant so much to me. It was a desire I didn't know I still wanted fulfilled in my life. I love my God because of it. Sometimes, the outcome of our battles is simply for God to get the glory out of our lives.

After completing my degree, I also completed my state licenses in life, health, and wealth management. So, in the short span of a year, I began to put a plan in place to move into another career path. But I still had questions about my health. I felt it was unresolved, and

I wanted to find out what and how I might have gotten so ill. I do remember when I was in the hospital, they discussed with me that the infection had come from some form of dental procedure, and now that I had some greater insight into the law and how to figure out if I was at fault or if someone else could have mistreated my conditions, I had my basis for my research, and I had the right mental tools to do the right research. The more time went by, the more I remembered. My mind went back to the previous time I felt this way, and the Holy Spirit reminded me of the dental visit.

So, I just started all this research into what constitutes malpractice. Who knew that having gone to law school was going to benefit me in this way?

I started scrambling, trying to figure out who could represent me. I called at least five to ten law offices with no success. Not because I didn't have a case but because I had not yet identified the source.

I thought it was the emergency room doctor from the hospital because while at the hospital, they couldn't really figure it out. Then, I began with my primary doctor, but I would later discover that I was looking at the wrong person.

There wasn't anything showing up on the X-rays. I was stuck. So, I did what I knew to do…I prayed. And God answered my prayer! God started leading me to different people that I didn't know.

There was one attorney who declined to help, but not before making a referral for another attorney.

After talking with me for a little while and learning that I was part of the Chargers organization, an attorney whom I never met put me in touch with the next person. But before meeting the next office, I went to the hospital and made a general inquiry into my records—no explanation provided, as I didn't want to tip my hand. I had to be wise and strategic.

God was guiding me.

I ended up at this large firm, and one of the associates went over my medical records...all 2,000-plus pages of them, at no charge, which is unheard of.

He gave me more clarity, but still no answer to the source, so I moved on from them, as they declined to help. However, the more information I received, the more confident I became in the possibility of having a malpractice case.

After about two months of research, I got an email from the office where the person who helped me because he was a fan of the Chargers, and he asked me to contact him immediately. He stated that I was on his heart and he really wanted to help, so he sent all my information to a colleague who was able to identify the needle in the stack of needles! He exclaimed, "We found it!"

I had *prevotella melaninogenica*; that's what the disease is called, and it's a rare disease that is formed in the mouth and causes one to go into sepsis shock. He told me it was my dentist, and he advised me to retain a lawyer specializing in dental malpractice immediately.

So, I called the large firm that I had first consulted prior to having this knowledge, but there was no answer. There was a sense of urgency to sign on the dotted line because the day this was discovered was the last day to file the lawsuit because of the statute of limitations. (This law gives you a certain amount of time from an injury to submit a lawsuit.)

So, I looked up some dental malpractice offices and came across a smaller firm that would decide to take on my case and represent me.

But wouldn't you know it? Not five seconds after the agreement was inked with the smaller firm, the larger law firm called me back and explained that they received my message and wanted to take my case. I had to decline, and they wished me luck.

So, it was time to get a plan and strategy. My lawyer made the declaration that we needed to gather all of the information to present a case. But remember, I was not working, and I had already done that legwork.

He said he would pay for the information needed to present my case.

But it wasn't long before it seemed as if the steam went out of the sails with regard to my case, and all of a sudden, he was very busy with others.

It was as if my case was insignificant or unimportant, so I had to do the paralegal work.

I may even go so far as to say that he didn't care, but since I had not taken the bar exam, there was only so much I could do. I couldn't file any motions or evidence.

I just went through law school and graduated, but I knew I didn't have the proper experience to actually file everything. I was at the mercy of my attorney to get things to the proper people at the right time. Eventually, I was facing the doctor who failed to identify the infection that was growing and threatening my life.

The dentist's response to my lawsuit was that he told me about the infection. I contested adamantly because I remembered my exchange with him verbatim. Besides, I had gathered all the proof that there was no referral to have my infected tooth pulled. There was no documentation in my medical records from him that he identified the condition to me.

I was gathering all this information for two years. Since my lawyer was just him in his private practice, we were like David against the legal Goliath. My case was easily worth a lot of money because of my economic worth, almost losing my life, and also the permanent damages to my physical, mental, and financial abilities to regain my normal life. But it wasn't about the money for me; it was about fighting for justice, fighting also for how our culture is treated when it comes to being mistreated in the medical world. We are seemingly always taking a hit! The law is made to compensate anyone who is wronged, and it is our right to sue to right a wrong. As an American and because of my education in law school, I now understood that I could pursue this in court without having some guilt trip. I talked it out with those close to me. Simultaneously, I was healing while fighting for myself. I had to fight my lawyer a lot as well, but I continued to fight for myself.

I was paying for things with my limited income from disability for things my attorney promised he would take care of, like witnesses, medical bills, filings, and such. Moreover, he would make me feel as if he didn't really believe in me or the case. He doubted the legitimacy of the source of my infection, too, so I had to remind him constantly of the evidence from my infectious disease doctor and all the evidence we were uncovering. He seemed to just be dragging his feet.

As a result of my faith, I was graced to be able to find the witnesses, and I found the expert witnesses I needed. Even the opposing lawyer told my attorney how impressed he was with me after my personal deposition.

This case was bringing things out of me I didn't know I had within. I was in a dark place, battling depression.

I was going through all kinds of stuff during these two years. I was in chronic pain, getting brain MRIs and experiencing anxiety and therapy all at the same time. It became so stressful at one time that I even had to fight off thoughts of suicide. I was walking through depositions with the knowledge in my mind that my lawyer still didn't believe me. How could I win this?

But you know what? I stood on God's Word, and I began to witness to my attorney. I told him that no matter what he did or didn't do...my God was going to come through for me!

They knew I was a Christian by the way I walked and talked. One of the main reasons for a deposition is to establish a plumb line for character.

I knew that if they couldn't get anything else, they would try to destroy my character. No matter how impressive they may have been, it was still their job to get their guy off, so that's what they were going to do.

Going through this lawsuit and not being able to work was hard for me. I had run out of savings, and I was on limited income until we finally got to the trial in March of 2023. That was three years after the onslaught of the infection and two years from my initial filing of the suit.

I didn't want to go through this process. I actually wanted to settle. But my lawyer was intimidated by the size of the opposing firm and just couldn't handle the pressure.

I actually experienced going through a whole case and can now see why God allowed it.

I got all the facts. I had the support of the Chargers and other great character witnesses. I had all these great people backing me as I approached the trial date. It's one thing to learn the law and another to experience it personally.

It was tough to relive the whole thing. It was tough to control and hold back my tears because there were pictures on the big screen in the courts of the gash and the hole in my chest, and the photos showed my body open down to the bone as if you could see through my body. I had to relive the trauma yet again... I was sitting next to the jury, trying to read their faces, and the dentist had a solemn look on his face as I believe he didn't know he caused so much damage. I was going through all this mental anxiety from the trial, and I was shaking. I wanted that to be because of the cold temperature, but it was coming from the inside of me.

My body was tense and tight as it was my turn to give testimony. I was called under oath. This was not a joke! And not just me. My parents and friends were giving character testimonies.

We got to a point in the case where it was clear the other side was caught in untruths and inconsistencies.

My lawyer finally started to believe that our evidence and facts held true during the trial when the case was unfolding; he leaned over and said, "We got them now!"

How? We finally found a 3D image of my mouth that showed the problem missed by the dentist. It looked like an open-and-shut case from that time forward. During a recess, my lawyer and I went into the restroom and checked under all the stalls for privacy. I remember it feeling like a scene from a crime drama or movie.

We were on the last day right before closing arguments, and we felt confident that we would win this, but I also knew anything could happen. He began to see aspects of the case that were not lining up. It felt like he finally believed me, but was it too late? Was his lack of zeal from the beginning going to impact the outcome?

After my legal team listened to the testimony of my parents and my sister Letrice, he opened up a lot to me after we did our team debrief.

No one knew about my desire to host my own Christian podcast at this point because I didn't say anything. But my dad said something about it, and it was visible that it left a good impression in the courtroom. After my dad got off the stand, I could feel the pride he had in me.

The closing arguments came, and my lawyer presented all the evidence, the lies, and cover-ups from the dentist's office that would strengthen our stands. This was where it got crazy. The defense lawyer stood up and said, "You know what? I believe," as he pointed at me, "that this African-American man is so smart that he's manipulating the system. He is a mastermind. I believe that he went to school to learn the law just so he could cheat the system and get money from my client."

Now, mind you, I could have asked for a lot more money, but I didn't. I asked for what was fair and even below my economic worth. As he continued this kind of assault on me, he included a disingenuous cry; he pushed out tears in order to pull the emotions of the jury. My dad, my sister Letrice, my brother Chris, and one of my nephews came to the closing arguments. They physically witnessed him saying these things about me.

There were times during the trial that the dentist would make facial expressions that appeared to reflect remorse for what he had done to me, almost an acknowledgment and apology. He would sometimes look over at my family as well.

It was then time for the jury to deliberate. It is usually said that the longer they deliberate, the better, but one hour before the deadline that would take us into the next day, they called us in for the verdict.

When I first got into the courtroom before they read the verdict, I prayed to God and just said, "Let Your will be done." In a civil suit, you just have to win by majority vote. They came into the courtroom, and of course, we all stood up as they read the two-part verdict, and to both mine and my lawyer's surprise, the judge read the verdict that he did not commit malpractice. I put my head down, not in defeat but to process what had just happened. I didn't cry, I didn't go off, but Letrice got up and walked out. My dad let out a gasp, and even the court reporter who was sitting in front of me just put her head down.

Here I was again, having the ability to win but getting knocked down in my face. It wasn't just about the money; I wanted justice. I didn't want anyone else to go through this, and it is the obligation in the medical field to make sure professionals are careful, and this guy wasn't careful. He may not be a bad person, but he was negligent. He got caught up in what I did and didn't consider who I was.

A man. A father. A son. A brother. He didn't really take care of me. I don't think that he really knew what he really did to me and how he affected my life.

The judge polled the verdict count. The mostly White, middle-class jury chose the defense for their votes. The non-White jurors, who were outnumbered, voted for me.

The judge made an announcement that everyone was clear to discuss the case on social media and asked whether anyone had any feedback about the case. Some members of the jury began to laugh about it in my face, and while I sat there and took the verdict professionally, they gave feedback on how they wished they got paid more for their time and made jokes and laughed, and I had to sit through it.

My lawyer was livid and in shock at their behavior and insensitivity. Even the judge joined in and made tactless comments. I wanted to interject and address the courtroom so badly, but I was aware of my surroundings, too. I said to my lawyer, "What is going on here? I have to sit through this?" He just said, "Hold it, don't make an interruption," because their uncaring banter could create problems for me. I didn't even give them anything. It was clear that it was expected of me as a Black man to get indignant and out of the very character that was testified that I had.

When it was time to face the opposing counsel, my flesh wanted to reject the extended hand gesture to shake mine, but I did what a man would do, and I obliged, only to the lawyer. I did not shake the dentist's hand.

My lawyer asked if I wanted to find out why the jurors decided on their verdict. I told him he could follow up with me on that. I was just ready to leave the courtroom as the trial was ten days long, and I had gone through this for two years. I was tired and just wanted to rest.

When I got home, I didn't even cry; I just went straight to my room and had a talk with my God. I told

Him that I loved Him. I told Him that I loved Him a lot for all that He helped me learn about myself and how to stand my ground when every arrow was shot at me. I learned in the process. I just didn't want to talk to Him or anyone about the case right now. The case is over, and it is what it is. I was not angry; I just wanted to sleep.

I woke up the next day, and I felt different. I had slept sideways, and I didn't feel any sharp pains in my arm. I could raise my hand, and I was able to move it above my head! For the past two or three years, I could not do this function. I had been taking pills just to sleep with no pain. At first, I didn't tell anybody.

Before this miracle moment, I couldn't even grab a grocery bag. I even demonstrated at the trial the damage that was done to my arm.

I went downstairs, and I FaceTimed everybody, checking in on their well-being, and everyone was still upset about the verdict. My family knew I had every right to take time to recover from what they witnessed, but I reassured them that I was okay, and I let my family know that it was time to move on and let it go. I understood that there are other people worse off than me. There are people incarcerated but innocent, like me, but I didn't go to jail. That is why I couldn't cry over the verdict.

I didn't complain to God even though I went through so much because I trusted Him so much!

I could look back and see that God was possibly saving me from potentially years of the attorneys for the dentist appealing any financial award and trying to tie my life up in the court system.

That morning, before I went downstairs, I heard God tell me, "Finish the book!" He reminded me of the words from the judge that there was no NDA (non-disclosure agreement) about the content of the trial, and by this time, I had stopped writing the book midway to concentrate on the trial. Over the next five days, I worked nonstop around the clock on the book. I wrote in the neighborhood of about 20,000 words. I just let it go. I still hadn't told anyone that my arm had healed until a week or so later.

Soon after, my dad and I had this conversation surrounding all that had happened. My dad said, "I've seen some prejudices in my life, but your trial opened my eyes to this type of racism." He continued to tell me how he was proud of me battling and fighting, and from that conversation came the book title.

The word "battered" was in my head, but as I asked him if it is battered or battled from the scripture in the Bible, he said battered, but we both thought at once "battled" is a better term for the title and it resonated with me, so I went with it.

At this point, I didn't have any more checks left. I didn't have any more money. I was done. I mean, I paid for these lawyers, and I paid for all this stuff. With all these kinds of things that were going on, I was flat broke. My dad continued to reiterate in our conversation that people will invest when you can fully explain what they are in investing in, not just a plan, but whether the plan has been put in motion.

Soon after, I saw an ad from TBN looking for Christian authors, and at first, I thought it was a scam, but I was encouraged to send in my manuscript. I soon had an interview and was asked to give a summary of my story and send the entire manuscript that was completed at that time. I got an email back from the representative of Trilogy Publishing telling me how much they loved my book. He added that he could see how it would help so many people and give them hope, which is what this book is all about. I received a contract that day. I was so excited, and when I delivered the news to my loved ones, they, too, were so excited.

I quickly recognized God's love and His care for us to turn ashes into victory! The things that had happened to me, my battle, my bruises, and submitting to God finally brought me to the place where what *God* was going to do for me, no man, no court system was going to be able to get the credit for. I got the victory over them!

Until the writing of this book, I hadn't talked about the case. No amount of money could buy peace, my healing, and my deeper, intimate connection with my Creator! That is what I gained as a result. The court docket may mark the experience as a loss...but in the court of heaven, it is a grand W!

I can honestly say I'm glad it didn't work out and I didn't get the money. I gained the riches of God's favor, His divine healing, and His amazing grace! I didn't get bitter; I got better! I forgave the dentist for not being truthful and taking responsibility for his negligence. I went through this trial and realized it was less about the dentist and more about what God wanted to pull out of me.

I was battled, tested, and God approved, and I hope that whoever reads this is inspired to trust God to take all of their battles and every bruise and use it to show Him strong on their behalf, as He did for me.

CHAPTER 10

Place of Conflict to the Place of Calling

There is something about when God calls a ceasefire in your mind so that the healing of our wounds can begin.

It doesn't take away the memory of the battle or erase the scars, but what His healing balm of love, grace, and mercy does is restore, rejuvenate, and revive.

I woke up. I praise God. Life is still good. I have a "God, thank You!" on the inside of me. I went through all of it to receive patience, understanding, and grace.

I had a dream where God explained the purpose of why I went through the difficulties in my life. These experiences will help build the legacy I want to leave for my children and for those around me whom God has put before me. I know it may sound off, but I am actually glad that God allowed me to go through it all and that it all ended the way it did. It taught me endurance, long-suffering, and patience. I became a more loving and understanding man. I thank God that my kids saw me be strong through the battles and rise above the bruises.

My youngest would remind me of what it was like for him to see me rise out of the slumps I was in, and I am their Superman. It felt like I was in a swampland or quicksand, swatting mosquitoes and pushing my way through the bushes, moving through dark, murky waters. That was my path to get to "there"!

But now that I have come out on the other side, I can show others the way out. Like Jesus did for me, I can leave my footprints to help guide others out of the darkness. I was built for my path from before the foundation of the world and I come from a legacy of strong overcoming men and will leave the same and greater for my sons and others to follow.

"God is not playing puppet." That's what my dad says all the time. God has purpose for all that He allows. God is not playing with your life, on the contrary, He is helping you to navigate through it. He knows the way... He planned it. Even when I didn't know where my path would lead me, I trusted in the One who orchestrated it.

I wanted more than anything to be able to hear God's voice and know it intimately. That desire costs.

Some people learn with a chisel, some learn with a hammer, and others learn with a jackhammer. My lessons came like a wrecking ball, but I overcame them!

Revelation 12:11 (KJV) says, "And they overcame him by the Blood of the Lamb, and by the word of their testimony and they loved not their lives to the death."

The devil tried to kill me, he tried to steal from me, and he attempted to destroy me...*But God!*

I have met so many people along the way, and I have heard many testimonies of the different paths our lives can take. The stories can help us grow in confidence that we are not alone and that we can help each other heal with the power driven from communications. The true inspiration for this memoir. I declare as long as I have breath in my lungs, no matter the battle, no matter the bruising...I will keep declaring the awesome goodness of God!

About the Author

I Am Here to Serve You, My God, No Matter the Cost!

Tray, a native of Oceanside, CA, is the son of Clarence and Josephine Crayton Jr., the second youngest of five children.

Tray is a former professional athlete, and after retiring from football, he began a career working in sales and brand marketing. He has worked for very prominent franchises such as 24-Hour Fitness and the Los Angeles Chargers, to name a few, before founding his company, Turn Up Wealthy, a brand consulting business.

His current projects at the time of this writing are "Triumph with Trai," a podcast, and "In the Huddle with God," a Christian-based vlog, a platform that focuses on mental health and triumphing through life's challenges.

Tray discusses topics that are based on his own journey with Christian principles, which were usually experienced in three major areas of his life…sports, faith, and love.

His goal is to help his community and the world at large heal and create victories in times of need.

In 2020, during the COVID-19 pandemic, Tray faced a challenging, rare disease that nearly took his life. He stands on the belief that without his Lord and Savior, Jesus Christ, and the love and support of his entire family, he would not be here today.

Tray states, "Looking death in the face really changes a human."

His purpose and passion are to band together with like-minded individuals and organizations to tackle the truth of God's Word and the deep issues of violent assaults that are spawns of mental illness.

It is his firm belief that together, we can uplift others and encourage them in their efforts to battle and overcome their fights with depression, anxiety, and social injustices in our world today.

This book takes a deep dive into his emotional and inspirational journey. His hope is to enlighten readers to understand that we can make it through the most unconscionable events, deal with our questionable decisions, and obtain victories that help us navigate through life both in the face of failures and successes.

Tray believes with the power, purpose, and wisdom from the experiences we share, we gain hope and we can impact our communities.

The most important thing in his life is his personal relationship with and belief that with and through Jesus Christ, we can do all things!

Tray is passionate about serving others and with his God-given talents in sports, branding, sales, marketing, and the art of public speaking. And he is committed to finishing the race assigned to him from above. His dedication to helping and serving is an extension of his love for God, his family, and his city!

Printed in the USA
CPSIA information can be obtained
at www.ICGtesting.com
LVHW012307100824
787895LV00011B/302